A Tale of Two Tigers

Princeton's Historic Consolidation

Chad Goerner

Table of Contents

Dedication

This book is dedicated to all of Princeton's elected officials, volunteers and members of the League of Women Voters who have fought for consolidation since 1952. The battle for uniting Princeton Borough and Princeton Township comprised numerous skirmishes over the course of six decades, but finally the efforts culminated in victory.

Your contributions made it happen.

I also thank Pam Hersh, who, as a solider in past consolidation campaigns, enthusiastically lent her writing and editing talents to this manuscript.

Forward

The consolidation of Princeton Borough and Princeton Township is a ray of light in the darkness of New Jersey's fiscal and governmental woes. It is not only a story for New Jersey, but also a story that parallels the challenges facing New York, Pennsylvania, Missouri, Iowa, Massachusetts, Illinois and many other states grappling with the costs of local government.

How do people get so identified with the borders of their town that they are unable to even discuss municipal consolidation?

The inefficiency of hundreds of separate, redundant taxing districts makes it extremely difficult for states to: address planning and regional services; lower property taxes; and modernize the delivery of virtually every essential service.

How did the Princetons overcome their own history of failed attempts and the difficulties of combining their two towns?

Leadership.

Chad Goerner was that leader. As a candidate for local office, he ran with the stated goal of consolidating the Princetons. As an elected official he formed relationships and worked closely with the borough to make sure the process began on solid footing and continued to fruition.

While serving as mayor, Chad also served as a commissioner on the Princeton Joint Shared Services and Consolidation Commission and remained laser focused on his mission to combine the two municipalities. After the community voted to consolidate, Chad served on the Transition Task Force that was tasked with taking the uncharted steps to dissolve two incorporated towns and form a new one.

Many residents, elected officials and employees worked just as hard for the success of this effort, but Chad Goerner was its leader throughout the process. He now has written a tale to inspire other towns to move toward consolidation.

Princetonian Albert Einstein said that "the definition of insanity is doing the same thing over and over again, but expecting a different result." As you will read, the two Princetons' multi-decade attempts at consolidation were insane and stressful – but the out-of-the-box thinking led them to initially share services and then grow together and ultimately consolidate.

This book is about their unique history of shared services and efforts to consolidate that on the fourth attempt in 2011 realized a different result.

My organization, CourageToConnectNJ is a non-profit, non-partisan organization whose purpose is to educate the public about the impact of "Home Rule." We provide venues for engagement and present a model for connecting communities' administrative structures including fire districts, school districts, police departments and municipal governments. Princeton has proven that when local governments collaborate and innovate, they can become more efficient and effective resulting in improved planning and responsiveness.

With the right combination of state leadership and financial support, local governments in New Jersey and in other states can benefit from restructuring through service regionalization and consolidation. We look forward to working with them to help them achieve real results similar to what the Princetons have achieved.

Gina Genovese
Executive Director
CourageToConnectNJ

Prologue

Local governments across the country are responsible for responding to emergencies, protecting their citizens, repairing roads and even licensing dogs. In many cases there are simply too many local governments to deliver these services efficiently and effectively. While this is a national problem, New Jersey and neighboring New York are particularly struggling with how to deliver efficient and effective services in light of stagnant tax revenues, increasing costs of goods and services, and their states' two percent spending cap.

New York and New Jersey both have their own issues with municipal government inefficiency. New Jersey has 565 municipalities and 599 school districts. New York has more than 10,521 taxing districts resulting in a lasagna-like layer of multiple tax bills and resultant inefficiency. What's the solution to this morass of home rule? Both states have taken action to make it more feasible for residents and elected officials to consolidate towns and school districts. Success has been led from the bottom up in New Jersey, with Princeton being the first major local government merger in over a century. In New York State, however, the governor's office has been proactive in encouraging more local government mergers, service sharing and innovation from the top down.

In 2011, after six decades of failed attempts, Princeton Borough and Princeton Township consolidated to form a single town. Many visitors to Princeton have no idea that the town used to be two separate towns. Residents themselves may know this, but many of them are even unaware of exactly where the borders of the former Princeton Borough and Township began and ended.

Because of the many failed efforts and the successful 2011 effort, Princeton offers local governments a unique case study on what can go right after a lot of trying and failing.

The consolidation of Princeton now has reached its mapped-out 'full implementation,' three years after the consolidation took effect in 2013. Data have shown consolidation to be successful at not only significantly reducing costs and slowing tax increases (Princeton has one of the slowest tax growth rates in all of Mercer County, New Jersey since consolidation), but also fostering improved planning, crisis response and communications for the town's 30,000 residents.

I wrote this book to provide an account of the historic consolidation of Princeton Borough and Princeton Township. Out of all the communities in New Jersey, Princeton has had the most comprehensive test of consolidation and shared services in the state and perhaps in the nation. Its history provides a look into the challenges and pitfalls of such efforts.

Looking back 60 years gave me a better understanding of what transpired, what went right, what went wrong, and ultimately what helped formulate a successful consolidation effort.

In addition, I wanted to outline how we approached and completed the consolidation so that Princeton's process could serve as a model for other towns throughout the country. Princeton's attempts, the unsuccessful ones and the final success with the 2011 referendum vote, provide an historical and political insight presented in this book. It gives the elected official, concerned citizen or state legislator a structural framework drawing from Princeton's collective experience.

Multiple governing units contribute to duplicate services and higher costs of government. But equally detrimental is that this layered governing structure fails to aid our residents in attaining cohesive strategic planning for development, transportation and infrastructure improvements.

In order to have 'smart growth,' New Jersey has to have smarter, more efficient government. To accomplish this, New Jersey must be more proactive in its efforts to encourage consolidation and shared services at the state level. When Princeton first applied for a consolidation and shared services commission study grant, the NJ Department of Community Affairs was able to provide a matching grant to help fund the cost of the commission's consultant. Those funds currently are unavailable for towns looking to study consolidation and/or shared services. The lack of funding for information gathering thwarts municipalities from getting started on the process. In addition, the legislature should consider additional reforms to the municipal consolidation law to make it even easier for towns to study consolidation.

It takes creative and open-minded officials to look beyond the short-term goal of getting re-elected and to consider examining what might be best in the long term for the community by utilizing consolidation and shared services to make government more efficient and more effective. A consolidation or shared service effort only will be successful through leadership. This book provides an historical blueprint to help guide those willing to lead.

Princeton's success with consolidation would have been unattainable without dynamic and involved residents and volunteers, the governing officials and perhaps most importantly the municipal staff. While many of them were concerned about their own job security and benefits packages, the municipal staffers bravely shepherded the implementation and helped make it a success. Princeton was and is blessed with many selfless volunteers that contributed countless hours to the consolidation effort. This was a collective, community effort and the results speak for themselves.

Glossary

Home Rule

Steve Adubato, Ph.D. in an op/ed for NJTV defined it simply and effectively. *"Home rule," as it is called, is the belief that every town, city or borough has a right to have its own police department, fire fighters, water system, planning director and its own school system – no matter how big or small the municipality or how much it costs." [http://www.njtvonline.org/perspectives/op-ed-an-end-to-nj-home-rule/; September 1, 2011]*

Home Rule is one of the key reasons that states like New Jersey struggle with multiple layers of government. It represents local control and is mistaken for community identity – preventing many local officials and state legislators from making progress in improving planning, service delivery and controlling costs.

Consolidation

In New Jersey consolidation and shared services are usually mentioned in the same conversation, yet they are different. Consolidation is the full merging of two or more local governments into a single entity. With that comes a combined administration, a single governing body, a single planning board and all services (police, public works, etc.) delivered under one governing umbrella.

While it can lead to budgetary cost savings, like it did with the Princeton consolidation, the municipalities reap other benefits from consolidation.

- ***Strategic planning - The combined town can synergize its planning for the future.*** In New Jersey, many communities are inter-related, and some are surrounded by another town. As was the case with Princeton Township and Princeton Borough, the borough was the donut hole and the township was the surrounding donut.

Decisions regarding traffic, zoning and development could be made by the township that would ultimately affect the borough and vice versa. Yet, without a consolidated governing body, residents from either municipality may get boxed in literally and figuratively by losing their say on and control over a planning/development initiative.

- ***Infrastructure - Infrastructure improvements can be significantly enhanced and streamlined with consolidation.*** Coordinating sidewalk construction, road improvements and bike lane installation may sound easy for two towns, but when that decision is made by two engineering departments, two advisory committees and two governing bodies, it may never happen or it will almost certainly take much longer to get done.

- ***Emergency services - Consolidation can dramatically improve emergency response in times of crisis.*** As mayor during Hurricane Irene and Hurricane Sandy, I saw firsthand how two towns provide a slower and disjointed response compared to a unified one. A unified town with a single plan of action can free roadways sooner and respond to residents in a more coordinated and proactive fashion.

Consolidation may not be the solution for all municipalities and school districts, but for some it is certainly worth considering. It has the potential to create a more sustainable budget that can survive under the states' two percent municipal budget cap without drastically reducing surplus or cutting valuable services. In fact, it has the potential to enhance services as Princeton has proven.

Shared Services

Shared services are individual services or departments that are shared between two or more towns.

Most elected officials talk about shared services instead of consolidation. Why? Home Rule. A shared service still lets the elected officials keep their jobs and maintain control, and it is not as intrusive, final, and comprehensive as consolidation. Many towns have shared services, but many only share the small departments of services that are less controversial and save a negligible amount of money. Officials with an eye towards re-election generally avoid tackling the hot button and complex issues of sharing the big-ticket departments, such as police and/or public works.

However, there are exceptions that prove that shared services and consolidation really do make sense when there are open-minded elected officials that make it happen. Chester Township and Chester Borough, as of this writing, have entered into a shared police service where Chester Township will assume the authority and absorb the borough's former police department. This will save money and most likely lead to service improvements for the towns' residents.

Shared service police departments can fail to materialize, however, as there are fears of one town losing control over the police function. The cases of shared police services in New Jersey almost always involve one town giving up their police force and contracting with the other town for service.

Alternatively, towns can create an extra bureaucracy known as a "joint meeting" and give police an unclear line of communication between the joint meeting and the governing bodies. As of this writing there are no joint-meeting police forces in the state of New Jersey. In Princeton, for example, the township police department made it clear that its biggest concern about a shared-service police force was the absence of a clear chain of command.

Furthermore, shared services sometimes can create additional layers of bureaucracy unless just one municipality is in control. In cases where there is joint control, they tend to be governed by a joint board and this can serve as a way for one governing body to grandstand against the other. Before Princeton Borough and Princeton Township became one town, the two towns shared about 13 different services.

Princeton's Consolidation Timeline

1952 - The Consolidation Report of The League of Women Voters of the Princeton Community is presented to the community recommending consolidation.

1953 – The Princeton Joint Consolidation Committee is formed as a result of the League of Women Voters report. It recommends consolidation, however, voters of both municipalities reject consolidation that November.

1962-1965 – The Joint Commission on Municipal Operations is formed to review potential collaboration between the two towns on a departmental basis up to and including full municipal consolidation. They recommend additional collaboration including a regional health department and a joint regional planning board but stop short of recommending consolidation mainly because of divergent tax rates in the two municipalities.

1966 – Princeton Township and Princeton Borough successfully vote to regionalize their school system after the vote failed in the previous November in the borough.

1969 – The towns form a Joint Regional Planning Board.

1973-1976 – The towns form an advisory consolidation commission, the Princeton Joint Consolidation Committee. The committee concludes with a recommendation to consolidate, however, there is not a binding voter referendum due to the advisory nature of the commission. A vote is put on hold as the state legislature considered changes to the municipal consolidation law and the school funding formula.

1975 – The towns form a regional board of health, 10 years after it was recommended in the 1965 report.

1978-1979 – A formal commission is elected under the Municipal Consolidation Act. The Joint Municipal Consolidation Study Commission completed their work in 1979 and recommended consolidation. It failed in Princeton Borough by 33 votes.

1991 – A referendum is placed on the ballot in both the township and the borough to form a consolidation study commission. Princeton Borough rejects it.

1995-1996 – A formal commission is again elected under the Municipal Consolidation Act. The Joint Consolidation Study Commission recommended consolidation. It failed in the borough by a wider margin than the 1979 vote.

2009-2011 – A commission is formed under the Local Option Municipal Consolidation Act (2007) and is named the Joint Shared Services and Consolidation Commission (JSSCC). The JSSCC is charged with studying shared services (police and/or public works) or full municipal consolidation. The commission recommended full municipal consolidation. Wide margins in both municipalities approved the measure.

2012 – The year Princeton Borough and Princeton Township technically remained separate, but engaged in work to enable a single municipality on January 1, 2013.

2013 – First year of operation for the newly consolidated town known simply as Princeton.

2016 – Consolidation reached full implementation with the close of 2015. Savings exceeded JSSCC estimates.

PART ONE

Consolidation of Princeton Borough and Princeton Township

Sandy: Irene's Uglier Sister

"We are all over this Frankenstorm."

– **Princeton Administrator Robert Bruschi**, responding to an email from the mayor about the newly unified town's preparedness for the impending hurricane – October 26, 2012.

As October of 2012 began, Princeton Borough and Princeton Township were only three months away from officially merging into one town. They were learning how to navigate the choppy waters of togetherness that would result in the new entity to be known simply as "Princeton." The governing body was taking shape and I, no longer running for re-election to the office of mayor, had a final opportunity in my last months to hand off the reigns. I announced that instead of seeking another term, I would "guide the towns through to a successful consolidation without political distraction." Little did I know that my work as mayor - rather than my work as a consolidation facilitator - was still unfinished.

I woke up on the morning of October 26, 2012 to a Princeton administrator's email, entitled "Frankenstorm." Another email arrived shortly thereafter from the office of New Jersey Governor Chris Christie, who would be holding a conference call on the hurricane that was readying its wrath for New Jersey. And wrath was an understatement – Hurricane Sandy caused about $60 billion worth of damage throughout the state and left over 90,000 Mercer County residents without power [*The Times of Trenton*, "Mercer County residents without power struggle to stay warm during Nor'easter," November 8, 2012].

Princeton, while suffering less severely than the shore towns, nevertheless was in crisis – the power was out for over a week in many places of the town. Many roads were blocked with debris making it very challenging, if not impossible, for emergency services to reach our residents.

Princeton Borough and Princeton Township were officially still two towns. This was known as our "transition year." The Princetons were engaged, and the actual marriage or consolidation would occur in January of 2013.

However, we began to work together as one town in anticipation of being consolidated. This meant that we would have a joint Emergency Operations Center (EOC). The EOC was a way for us to work together to come up with a plan to prioritize clearing roads, assess problems with electricity restoration, and formulate communications to our residents. Rather than having two towns operating separately and working at cross purposes, we were working for the first time ever as a single, united municipality. It was making a difference.

Like most of the residents in town, I had no power. Unshaven and without a shower, I attended the opening of the center. All around me, the center was bustling with leadership from the now unified police force, administration, engineering and representatives from Princeton University and the school district. For the first time, we had a joint reverse 911 calling system for the towns to alert residents of shelter locations and other issues as a result of Sandy.

A large dry-erase board was set up in the front of the room to list problem areas and prioritize the roads that needed to be cleared of trees and debris to allow electric company workers to get through town and help restore power to our residents. The engineering department, led by Robert "Bob" Kiser, gathered call information from residents reporting power outages and relayed the information to Public Service Electric & Gas (PSE&G) which maintained the list of reported outages. The police monitored road clearing, traffic issues and resident concerns. These efforts would go on for the next week to make sure that power was restored throughout the community.

We decided to open a shelter where residents without power could shower, charge their phones, and get some rest, food, and warmth, particularly important because it was getting cold outside. Both Princeton University and the school district had facilities that could accommodate our residents, and their representatives on the EOC stepped up and offered space to shelter them if needed. As the power outages continued, the shelter and shower-access became critically important to our town. The integration of township, borough, university and school district personnel clearly contributed to the organized approach of working out from under Hurricane Sandy.

Election Day was approaching, and many of the polling locations that voters would utilize were without power and unable to function. The EOC, town administration and the representatives from Princeton University and the school district were working against the clock to reformulate locations for the upcoming elections. They succeeded in finding locations to accommodate all the voting districts, and the town handled the logistics to ensure that all voters could find their appropriate polling locations.

The departmental synergies were a stark difference from the response during Hurricane Irene in 2011. In previous years, the towns would communicate, but the public works departments were deployed separately. The towns battled storms and responses from within their own bubble. For example, when the region's hospital was located on the Princeton Borough/Township boundary on Witherspoon Street, township plows refused to plow the borough portion of Witherspoon Street during a blizzard, thus cutting off the crucial ambulance access route to the hospital emergency room.

In 2011, the two separate towns' response to Hurricane Irene was far less effective than the Hurricane Sandy response. Princeton resident Dr. Laura Kahn, a renowned public health expert, critiqued the Hurricane Irene emergency response effort in a letter to the editor of the Town Topics entitled "Hurricanes Do Not Recognize Political Borders:"

"To summarize my 10 years of study on crisis management in a sentence: unified leadership is vital for a community's safety. Princeton's leadership structure is poorly designed for crises. Princeton Borough is donut-holed within Princeton Township, a difficult arrangement from an emergency management, health and safety perspective. We have two separate police departments that must communicate and coordinate between two political entities during a crisis. Even worse, our elected officials, the people ultimately responsible for the health and safety of Princeton, are very much split. This cannot and should not continue. We need unified leadership. Putting the issue of consolidation to a public vote is a good first step in thinking and acting like one community. We are one community and here is our opportunity to prove it."

Over a month later in November of 2011, we did just that, and both towns voted to consolidate. In our transition year of 2012, the Superstorm Sandy effort was remarkably different from the Hurricane Irene effort. The improvements in response time and communication were unsurpassed.

With less than two months left in my term, I was filled with hope and optimism as the staffs from both municipalities were coming together. This is what consolidation was supposed to do, and united Princeton was setting an example. It was hard to believe that with the collaboration the towns exhibited during Hurricane Sandy that the two municipalities even had separated in 1813, and then failed to consolidate after six attempts over a period of 60 years.

The Separation and The Divorce

"Many residents of Princeton Borough firmly believe that the origins of the town are cloaked in nobility, and that this demi-Eden was designed by mystical forces..."

– **Alan Karcher,** New Jersey's Multiple Municipal Madness

To understand the statewide problem of having too many governing units, one must understand the origins of this governance structure. A renowned New Jersey legislative leader, Alan Karcher wrote a book *New Jersey's Multiple Municipal Madness* that offers a comprehensive look at how New Jersey ended up with 566 (565 after the Princetons consolidated) local governing units. The history of Princeton Township's and Princeton Borough's formation, separation and ultimate divorce gives a more granular look at how long ago municipal divorces created obstacles for future reconciliations.

The area that forms Princeton today was settled in the late 17th century. Princeton was governed in a limited fashion by the county governments having part located in Somerset and part under the auspices of Middlesex. Initially, the area was sparsely populated and remained so until the relocation of the College of New Jersey (Princeton University) to Princeton in 1756.

As the college grew and the surrounding area brought in more residents, traders and merchants, some locals became uncomfortable with unregulated alcohol consumption and wanted control of their own security. The county seats in New Brunswick (Middlesex) and Somerville (Somerset) were far away and could not provide the level of support that the locals felt they needed. By 1813, the town was hovering at around 700 residents.

A group of residents petitioned the legislature to incorporate a borough so they could gain control of the situation. However, their concept of 'security' was based on a goal to suppress African-Americans and regulate alcohol consumption.

The petition to the legislature stated "that on occasions, there are unlawful meetings of black people at improper hours for the purpose of drinking and carousing, to the manifest injury of the blacks themselves, their masters and employers – for the preventing further continuance and checking the growth of these vices – which you memorialists subscribe principally to the want of an efficient police – as well as to promote the due execution of the law."

The legislature agreed, and on February 11, 1813, the Borough of Princeton was created. While it would be semi-autonomous until 1894, the physical separation from the surrounding Princeton Township countryside was complete. During the formative years of Princeton Borough, the governing body moved slowly and struggled at forming a security force, mainly a sheriff, to provide the security in town. The governing body meeting minutes were focused on two objectives: granting permits for individuals to have taverns in their homes and figuring out how to regulate the African-American population.

Governing body minutes of July of 1817 showed the continued focus: "Misters Johnson and Green were appointed to a committee to frame an ordinance to prevent the riotous and tumultuous assemblage of Negroes within the borough." However, a year later it was still a key discussion at governing body meetings. From September 14, 1818: "The Recorder entered a complaint of some Negroes who had collected together, and disturbing the peace of the inhabitants by riotous proceedings conceived it necessary that some method be pursued to suppress this growing evil, which may be attended by serious consequences."

Two decades later in 1838, the area surrounding Princeton Borough, still largely an agricultural community, incorporated to form Princeton Township. The first meeting of "the Inhabitants of the Township of Princeton" was held in the Borough of Princeton, as the borough's formal separation would occur in 1894. Looking at the budget adopted at this first meeting, one can see that the township population was sparse and its governmental needs were minimal.

It mainly included:

- $500 for repair of the roads.
- $500 for support of the poor.
- $50 for the repair of all bridges.
- $400 for the Common Schools.
- a tax on each dog of one dollar ($1).

In 1894 Princeton Borough separated completely from Princeton Township joining many other new towns created through an unintended consequence of a law passed by the state legislature. They created a law giving incorporated towns the ability to control their own schools and the result was that many communities simply broke away and incorporated as their own town to control their own school district.

This resulted in a ballooning of municipalities throughout the state of New Jersey and socioeconomic separation as well. Many communities from the original town borders were left with lower income residents and fewer ratables to drive school construction.

The divorce was final. Princeton Borough existed on approximately 1.8 square miles and the surrounding, agrarian township occupied about 16.5 square miles.

Donut and Donut-Hole Community: *Princeton Borough at ~1.8 square miles, surrounded by Princeton Township at ~16.5 square miles. According to the 2010 Census, there were 12,307 residents in the borough and 16,265 residents in the township.*

At the local level each town went about its respective ways. But in the early decades of the 20th century, the towns began to share some services, the largest being sewer services for the borough and the more densely populated sections of the township.

In 1935, a Republican candidate for mayor named Charles Erdman, Jr., came forward. He was a member of the "Princeton Local Government Survey" – a group of prominent Princeton University professors and experts who examined New Jersey municipal governments. In announcing his candidacy for mayor in 1935, the short-lived Princeton newspaper, *The Local Express*, reported that "Mr. Erdman believes the economies in local government will be affected by consolidation of certain functions of government without the necessity of amalgamation of the various governing units. He points out that Princeton Borough and Township have led the way in this type of consolidation, by example, they have merged their sewage, garbage and fire protection services and...that further steps in this direction could lead to further savings." [*The Local Express*, "Incorporation of

Small Municipalities Termed By Erdman As 'Chronic Disease," October 24, 1935]

Mayor Erdman, elected in 1936, served for 10 years. The following year, the Princeton Local Government Survey, in which Mayor Erdman had participated, published a pamphlet entitled "Local Government in New Jersey: A Political Patchwork." It advocated for larger government units, since it contended that the then 564 municipalities were too many in number. However, it also pointed out the challenges of doing so and cited four main obstacles:

(1) Local pride and community consciousness.

(2) Inadequate legal authority.

(3) Widely varying school tax rates, debt service charge and tax delinquencies.

(4) Ultimate clashes between urban and rural districts. [*"Local Government in New Jersey: A Political Patchwork, Princeton Local Government Survey,"* Princeton University, 1937]

During his time in office, Mayor Erdman recognized that the planning and development of the Princeton community needed to be done as one town. Shared services alone never could address the joint planning and development needs of the broader community. In later years, he wrote in support of the first consolidation attempt and provided insight into the later 1930s challenges of development and the potential for unwanted industry in the fast-growing township. He recalled the challenges of failing to plan as one community.

"Such sound planning for our community can, in my opinion, be achieved only through actual unity. Some may talk of cooperation and bow politely, but let's face the facts. Back in 1937, the borough invited participation and waited months in vain hope for the establishment of a joint borough-township planning board. The same invitation was repeated without success in 1946, when a post-war building boom was looming large. In 1948 mutual invitations to attend each other's planning board meetings led to negative results. Finally, when the borough drew its master plan map of major streets, approach and by-pass roads, the official township reaction was that this mapping overstepped the proper functions of borough planning. The township planners insisted that the traffic problem of the community was no business of the borough—a perfect example of blindness to the inter-relation between congestion of borough streets and road improvements in the surrounding area. Cooperation is a lovely theory but it just hasn't worked. We need real unity in our planning and zoning. This will be achieved only through concentrating authority in one body representing the entire community. That means one governmental unit for Princeton, not two." [*Town Topics*, "Why I Plan To Vote For Consolidation", October 4, 1953]

The community throughout the first four decades had segregated schools, led by the borough which had a larger population. In the borough, the all black school, Witherspoon, also served as a receiver school for the township African-Americans. It would remain so until 1947 when the Princeton Plan was implemented. The all-white Nassau School and all-black Witherspoon School were transformed into a single integrated schooling structure, whereby kindergarten through fifth-grade students went to the Nassau School, and the Witherspoon school taught those from grades six through eight.

Even though the younger children were schooled in separate, segregated schools until 1947, the high school, which was run by the Borough of Princeton had been integrated since 1915. Initially, the borough had the bulk of the students, but the township began to grow quickly with new businesses and residents with school-aged children made their way through the ranks and up into the high school – ultimately resulting in a growing number of township kids in the high school.

This began to create some concern among township residents who wanted to have a say in their children's schools because it was the Princeton Borough School Board that was responsible for decision making at the high school. The township paid its share of the public education costs on a per student basis but had no representation on the borough school board. Some felt it was time to look at bringing the towns together. It was 1952, 58 years since the final split.

Failed Attempts to Reconcile

"There is always a sadness in the passing of an era. The old days of the rural Princeton Township and the Borough were good ones which all who knew them remember with pride and affection and the record of which new residents respect. But a nostalgic wish for the past does not bring it back; nor does it make the institutions of the past adequate to the present."

The Consolidation Report of The League of Women Voters of the Princeton Community *(October, 1952)*

With the township's population rising and the school system still on residents' minds, the League of Women Voters in 1952 began a study to look at consolidating the borough and the township. The township was growing quickly: between 1940 and 1950, the population grew by 65 percent compared to just eight percent growth in the borough [*The Daily Princetonian*, "Town Finds New Topics of Discussion in Proposed Consolidation of Borough-Township Government." December 9, 1952].

The once rural township was becoming more densely populated, and the issues of schools and strategic planning were becoming more and more an integrated discussion between the two municipalities.

A particularly hot issue was the high school. The Princeton Borough School Board controlled it with no township representation on the board. This frustrated township residents who wanted a say in the high school, and the prospect of shared control worried some in the borough as the rising township population could incur a higher demand for school and municipal services.

The league began by presenting a vision and outlining the broad problems of the two separately governed but united communities:

"Although the boundary demarcating the once rural township from a more urban borough still exists, the character of the community has changed to the extent that large parts of the township are now as urban as the borough, and the two municipalities form a small, natural urban community of residents who live together and work together. Maintaining a boundary that has become artificial will not bring back the good old days; but it does make more difficult the provision of first-rate municipal services. Consolidation would make the tasks of local officials easier and more rewarding by giving them a rational area of administration and by eliminating pointless rivalries between the two parts of the whole."

The report outlined four goals of consolidation:

1) *Integrate governmentally a community that is integrated in other ways.*

2) *Permit intelligent and effective governmental planning for future needs of the Princeton community.*

3) *Provide a rational basis for the provision of local governmental services to a growing population.*

4) *Eliminate the causes of the divisive and destructive rivalry that now exists to some extent between the borough and the township.*

Shortly after the league published its report, a successful petition effort was started to form a study commission. Ultimately, 23.5 percent of borough voters and 24.2 percent of township voters signed petitions proposing a consolidation study. An official "Princeton Joint Consolidation Committee" was formed to review and develop a potential plan for the consolidation of the two municipalities. The study then would go to the voters of both municipalities in a referendum in November of 1953.

In May of that year, the commission presented its plan to the public. They recommended full consolidation to form a town simply known as 'Princeton' – dropping the borough and township designations. They continued their proposal by outlining criteria for the merger:

1) *All debt would be combined into the single municipality (during this time there was no state provision allowing it to be portioned to the former municipalities).*

2) *Except for the allowing the borough to issue parking improvement bonds not to exceed $2,000,000, no other debt could be issued until the formal consolidation of the municipalities.*

3) *All ordinances would remain in force for a period of 90 days, after which they would expire unless re-enacted.*

4) *The volunteer fire companies and first aid squads of the borough would become companies and squads of the new municipality on and after the date of consolidation.* [Town Topics, "Commission Announcement," May 1953]

Immediately after the report, the forces for and against consolidation began to organize. The effort moved slowly with many residents paying minimal attention until the fall of that year. This would have a negative effect on refuting rumors and claims that arose shortly after the report was issued.

The main pro-consolidation focus was on advertising in the local papers and letters to the editor. The Town Topics also had a 'For Consolidation' and 'Against Consolidation' viewpoint essay from residents in several newspapers that year. The pro-consolidation pieces focused on the tied sense of community and the need for common, strategic planning for the towns' combined future. The anti-consolidation forces centered on fears of bigger government and getting out-voted - a red herring used in every consolidation attempt from that time forward.

Both towns had concerns. In the borough, volunteer fire fighters worried that consolidation would bring a paid fire department. The paid fire department fear had no basis in fact and never was among the recommendations of the joint consolidation committee. Nevertheless, the fire department in the borough led the fight against consolidation. Denouncing the League of Women Voters' study on Consolidation as "The Women's Agreement," [*Town Topics*, November 1, 1962] many among the anti-consolidation forces were long-time Princeton Borough residents who wanted no change – adding fuel to the fire being fanned by the volunteer fire fighters.

The fire department paraded through town shortly before the vote with the firefighters in fire engines and cars driving through town and blaring their sirens and music in protest of consolidation. *The Daily Princetonian*, reporting on the event in the paper on November 3, said that there were banners that read: "Stop the foolish scheme! We've saved Princeton for 150 years, help save it now."

Spreading throughout the towns were fears of: a larger government entity; voting "dilution;" merging of the police forces; the issues surrounding school growth and control; plus a myriad of insidious rumors. All the unsubstantiated rumors prompted a "Rumor vs. Fact" column in the *Town Topics* just before the vote in October of 1953.

The paper was frustrated by the rumors overtaking the importance of making an informed voting decision. "In effect, an aura of governmental wastefulness has been foretold, with education costs mounting from unneeded schools; taxes soaring as thousands of dollars are appropriated for unwanted municipal services, ranging from miles of mandatory sidewalks to paid fire companies: and Princeton's own governing bodies (both borough and township) somehow totally supplanted by imported politicians with the worst instincts of big city ward-heelers." [Town Topics, October 25, 1953]

The column went on to dispel many of these myths, but by late October it was too late to counteract the effects of the rumor campaigns. The only serious attempts to dispel myths and reach out directly to the public occurred in the last 30 days before the referendum. But voters already had made up their minds. Both towns soundly rejected consolidation; in the borough, the vote was 1966 "No", to 1451 "Yes", and the township 1498 "No" to 863 "Yes" [Town Topics, November 8, 1953].

Pro Consolidation Ad - November 1, 1953, *Town Topics*

Report of the Joint Committee on Municipal Operations (1965)

It would be another decade before the municipalities would look to consolidate again. The 1953 vote left a lot of animosity, but the issue never died.

Late in 1960, more than six years after the last vote, The *Town Topics* posed its 'Question of the Week' asking Princeton residents: "With Consolidation again in the news, do you feel it would benefit Princeton?" [August 21, 1960] Overwhelmingly, the respondents from the borough and the township favored the idea. One newcomer to the borough commented: "I'm quite bewildered by this idea of two mayors, two police forces and so on. Why is this? Is there a rivalry between the two municipalities?"

In 1962 via a resolution of the joint governing bodies, the Princeton Joint Committee on Municipal Operations was formed to "study the desirability and feasibility of joint functioning of the municipalities in the several areas of municipal organization and endeavor (including public education), both with and without political integration; and to report its findings and recommendations to the governing bodies."

This mission statement outlined a flexible approach. If the towns decided that consolidation made no sense at that time, they could instead recommend sharing additional services. The commission's report would coincide with another report on potentially consolidating the township and borough school district. This subject had been intensely debated, because of the rise in the township population, coupled with the township having no say in the governing of the high school as it fell under the auspices of the Princeton Borough School Board.

While the 1965 committee was sympathetic to the consolidation of the governing bodies, the committee members determined that the divergent tax rates prohibited a merger at the time because it would result in an unequal treatment for one group of residents over the other. The township's tax rate was 34 percent higher than the borough's [Town Topics, "No To Consolidation," September 9, 1965]. The report explained this in its rationale:

"The Joint Committee believes that the consolidation of Princeton Borough and Princeton Township is not practicable at this present time. This conclusion stems principally from the wide difference between the equalized tax rates in the two municipalities. The Joint Committee has been advised that the New Jersey Constitution does not permit the establishment of different general tax rates in two parts of a consolidated municipality. Therefore, it would not be legally possible for residents of the (former) township to pay taxes at a higher rate than residents of the (former) borough in a consolidated municipality, even if such an arrangement was approved as part of a consolidation plan."

The committee's report and recommendations reflected the belief that with an eventual equalization of tax rates consolidation was not only feasible, but also politically and strategically important. Further progress brought the municipalities closer together by encouraging planning and health department collaboration. The towns eventually established a joint regional planning board in 1969, after initial rejection of the idea from the Borough of Princeton.

Establishing a joint health department took even longer. Six years later, Township Mayor James A. Floyd explored a health board merger with another town in 1971, as the prospects for merging with the borough "were dismal." He felt that a larger, regional health board would deliver "better health services and more state money." [Town Topics, "Health Board Merger?" December 23, 1971] The health departments merged in 1975 after much discussion and reservation. A letter to the editor of the Town Topics in 1979, however, reflected none of the negativity. It praised the 1975 merger of the health departments, because the newly merged department saved money and space while addressing the health needs of the entire town. Furthermore, said the letter writer, "its success provides a strong basis for anticipating a comparable success for a merger of Princeton Borough and Princeton Township into a single town of Princeton." [Town Topics, "Mailbox," October 31, 1979]

While the parents were angsting over getting married, the kids managed to find a way to hook up in the schools. The biggest local news of 1965 was the recommendation of a regionalized school district. Earlier in the year, the school boards voted to recommend school regionalization for the combined Princeton. The residents seemed largely in favor of the idea with 62 percent of borough residents favoring the idea and an even higher, 84 percent, for the township.

However, as the year progressed, the borough began to move more into the undecided column influenced by an opposition group called "Save Our Schools" that wanted to keep the school systems separate. On the other side of the argument, the township now had more students in the high school, but had no say in the governance of the high school as it fell under complete authority of the Princeton Borough School Board. The township residents were adamant that they either gain a say in the high school for their kids in the system or they would forge ahead and build their own school. In October, voters went to the polls and the borough, to the shock of many in the community, rejected the merger by 158 votes [Town Topics, October 14, 1965].

Many thought the issue was dead in the water and that the towns would have to find their own way forward separately. However, a concerted effort by residents to recruit new school board candidates and to better inform the community led to another referendum in June of 1966 – only eight months later. It passed 1510 to 1235 in the borough and 2296 to 196 in the township. [Town Topics, "Princeton 'Yes' To Merger," June, 23, 1966]

Report of the Joint Consolidation Committee of Princeton (November, 1976)

The stars – and the municipal tax rates - began to align.

A rate difference of 29 percent in 1964 moved to only a seven percent divergence in 1969, according to the New Jersey Department of Community Affairs report of 1969, updating the municipalities on the effect of taxes as a result of municipal consolidation. The report was completed at the request of Princeton Township Mayor Jack Wallace and Princeton Borough Mayor Henry S. Patterson. When the towns regionalized the schools in 1966, the funding formula would prove to be the hang up this time around despite the converging local tax rates. The _Town Topics_ summed up the challenge "Under the present valuation ratio formula, the Borough pays 38.75 percent and the Township 61.25 percent of a thin, 10 percent slice of the school budget. The remaining whopping 90 percent is paid for on the basis of pupil enrollment: 28.4 percent for the borough, 71 percent for the township. If the entire 100 percent of the school budget were shared by Borough and Township under that 38.75-61.25 percent formula, the borough's tax rate would leap up 97 cents while the township's would go down 52 cents This would be, needless to say, a rather tricky thing to sell to Borough voters." [_Town Topics_, January 9, 1969, "Consolidation?"]

Both mayors remained optimistic, however, expressing hope that the legislature would come to their aid in the event they decided to move forward.

The discussions continued in the early 1970s and eventually the governing bodies appointed five members plus one or more alternates to an advisory Princeton Joint Consolidation Committee in 1973. Again, the charge was to study the "desirability and feasibility" of consolidating to form a single municipality. They first met in the fall of 1973 and met on balance twice monthly throughout 1974. In 1975-1976 the work was on hold while the legislature debated several pieces of legislation, concerning consolidation as it related to both school districts and municipalities.

Their report, issued in the fall of 1976, concluded with a recommendation to consolidate but ultimately did not go to referendum because it was a non-binding commission. The state legislature was working to pass the Municipal Consolidation Act that would help clarify important consolidation-related issues. While this was 1976 and each decade prior there were some attempts at consolidation, the report included this quote:

"For years we have been moving toward a merger of governmental functions, so that by now only a few services are operated separately between the two municipalities. We do not recommend the merger of those remaining without consolidation, because of the problems inherent in having such merged departments (the police, for example) subject to the control of two governing bodies. It is our belief, however, that the merger of such remaining services, as well as the governing bodies themselves, can be accomplished through consolidation with a minimum of disruption and with significant improvements in efficiency."

The key take-away from this time period was the passage of the 1975 "Thorough and Efficient Education Law" that shifted from a per-pupil sharing cost for funding schools to an equalized valuation based on assessed property values. This shift, coupled with the converging tax rates, made consolidation all the more possible.

In 1978, the state legislature passed the "Municipal Consolidation Act," which created a more precise structure governing the process of studying consolidation. To that end, the towns created a Princeton Joint Municipal Consolidation Study Commission. Voters elected commission members in November of 1978. They issued a preliminary report in May of 1979 and a final report in July of 1979. The final report was titled "A Unified Princeton."

A Unified Princeton (July 1979)

The 1979 Joint Municipal Consolidation Study Commission report directly addressed the naysayers of consolidation, quoting the most common concerns: “But, they ask, could we not adequately meet the future and act cooperatively in our common concerns, while preserving the two separate governments, while preserving that which is familiar, and even dear, to so many of us? They fear a loss of access to government if there is to be consolidation. They fear that a single Princeton will be something far bigger than the sum of its now two small parts. They therefore ask, why is it desirable to change? Are there compelling reasons to change to a single municipal government?"

The commission responded, “However, we do not share these views. We believe that by consolidating under the borough form of government we can better preserve the style of government and quality of representation to which all Princetonians have been accustomed. In consolidating, we will continue to be a small town."

The key reason: “Only a consolidated municipality will be able to plan and direct any future development of Princeton in a way that will preserve and maintain the qualities of life that most of its citizens desire, those qualities that are associated with the concepts of a small town.”

The report recommended consolidation of the two municipalities outlining the following key factors advantageous to municipal consolidation of the borough and township:

1. *There will be better planning and direction toward our desired growth and development.*
2. *There will be no appreciable tax shift from one municipality to the other.*
3. *The assets and liabilities of the two municipalities are readily transferrable.*
4. *There will be better municipal services and administration and a stronger economic base.*

5. *The ordinances of the two municipalities are readily reconcilable.*

6. *There will be more effective use of time and energies of citizen volunteer participants in our government.*

7. *We will speak with a stronger voice and better advance our interests.*

The 1979 commission was a heroic effort on consolidation that essentially continued the towns' look at merging from the earlier commission that was formed earlier in the 1970s and also voted to recommend consolidation. As mentioned, the earlier effort was a non-binding commission, meaning that their recommendation would not be subject to a voter referendum. It was put on hold because the state of New Jersey was on the verge of passing an act to assist municipalities in clarifying municipal consolidation procedures. After its passage, another commission was formed and in 1979 it too voted to recommend consolidation and it would be a tremendously inclusive effort incorporating over 100 subcommittee volunteers. The 1979 report contained a significant level of fiscal analysis and clear recommendations that would later be utilized as a template in the 1996 consolidation commission effort.

Encapsulating the arguments for consolidation, residents David and Anne Reeves held an "On The Line" open house. Their home straddled the borough and township boundaries. They paid taxes in both municipalities and were unsure which police department to call in the event of an emergency. Billed as a "Party To Learn Why 'The Line' Is a Source of Constant Confusion," the informational event was targeting undecided 'on the fence' voters who were also 'on the line.' [*Town Topics*, October 17, 1979] At the open house, they served refreshments featuring donuts and donut holes, representing the township and borough, respectively.

The 'On the Line'/ 'On the Fence' theme was echoed by township resident Libby Shanefield in a letter to the editor a week later: "I live on Jefferson Road. My neighbors' kitchen is in the borough and their living room is in the township. Recently I called the township engineering department about dangerous potholes in front of my house. Township road workers told me that it was the borough's water gushing down the street that was causing the township's potholes. When there was a car accident at Franklin and Jefferson 100 feet away, I called the borough police. When a strange cat was stuck on a limb of my backyard pear tree, I called the township police. Then, there is the leash law! Borough dogs must be leashed at all times, but township dogs have to be home before 7 a.m. Perhaps township dogs can tell time better than borough dogs? In this area township houses look just like borough houses. Township people walk and bicycle around just like borough people. Are there any real differences that warrant keeping us separated so arbitrarily? From one who is 'on the line' to you who are 'on the fence,' -- please vote Yes for consolidation on November 6. End this divisiveness by voting for ONE Princeton." [*Town Topics*, "Letter to the Editor," October 24, 1979]

It also became apparent that the lack of coordination between elected officials and the consolidation commission could impact the vote. Only weeks before the consolidation vote, the township considered a bond ordinance to remodel existing buildings. This stoked fears that the borough could be responsible for that indebtedness. [*Town Topics*, "Remodeled Township Buildings Needed Whether or Not Consolidation Passes," October 24, 1979]

Princeton Township Mayor Josie Hall came out against consolidation and her statements against consolidation would eventually be used as some of the anti-consolidation arguments effectively undercutting the consolidation commission's work. This would serve only to add fuel to the anti-consolidation campaign.

The pro-consolidation campaign was a dedicated group that had pro-consolidation ads in every paper to combat the anti-consolidation ones in the weeks leading up to the election. The *Town Topics* Q&A on consolidation supplemented the ads; they made sure that certain facts were in front of the voters and a constant supply of letters to the editor promoting consolidation. Even the 1965 commission's members – six of the nine still living in Princeton -- wrote to voice their support for a 'yes' vote on the referendum, [*Town Topics*, October 31, 1979] along with all the major town newspapers the *Town Topics* and *The Princeton Packet.*

Needed in the last weeks of the campaign, however, was a proactive, rapid response to many of the myths and rumors circulating around town. The pro-consolidation groups discovered an anti-consolidation report being disseminated in the borough entitled "Analysis and Evaluation Review: Impact of Consolidation on Borough Residents." Commission members and pro consolidation residents made a valiant effort as they held a press conference to dispel the myths and misstatements in the report.

Calling it a "scurrilous document [that] falls just short of being a pack of lies," Princeton Borough resident William H Walker, continued: 'It is full of half-truths, misstatements, implications, statements out of context, and it raises questions already answered in the consolidation report.' For almost two hours, Mr. Walker; his co-chair Ingrid Reed; township co-chairs Stanley C. Smoyer and Martha Hartmann; and Jay Bleiman, a member of the study commission, went over the document point by point." [*Town Topics*, "Opposition's Paper is Termed Grossly Inaccurate," October, 24, 1979] The problem was that time was running out. It was October 24th - and the November referendum was rapidly approaching.

Still, both the pro and anti groups organized voter outreach efforts with district workers, captains and neighborhood representatives [*Town Topics*, "Consolidation's Fate to be Decided By Voters Next Tuesday," October 31, 1979]. This was the first time that a concerted get-out-the-vote effort was being made, and each side hoped it would favorably impact their cause.

The referendum failed by 33 votes in Princeton Borough, (total: 1479 for and 1512 against), the close vote prompting a recount and confirmation later in the month. This was a tremendous blow to the consolidation commission and the pro-consolidation group in the community. The amount of effort expended to research, analyze and recommend consolidation only to lose in the borough by 33 votes knocked the wind out of the consolidation effort for the next decade. But the commission did not go away quietly.

Couples Counseling

The commission responded immediately after the vote and published a "Concluding Report" that recommended closer cooperation with the goal of better governance and potentially a future consolidation of the two towns.

First, the commission recommended the formation of a Joint Municipal Coordinating Committee.

This committee would comprise both mayors, a member of each governing body, and the administrators of both towns. The goal was to ensure that issues facing the broader Princeton community would be communicated to the governing bodies and administration of both towns. The recommendation had three main tenets:

1. All issues to come before either governing body that may affect the other municipality would be placed on the agenda for the committee's meetings.
2. Minutes of these meetings would be distributed to all governing body members.

3. The mayors would alternate each meeting in serving as chair, and the administrators would alternate in serving as secretary.

The Concluding Report continued: "Through this formal means of mutual discussion, no action that affects the other municipality should be taken by either governing body without prior joint consideration and provision for resolution of potential conflicts."

After such a close vote, the bad feelings and tension festered between the two towns and the Joint Municipal Coordinating Committee never got off the ground. A frustrated, former 1979 commission member William Selden wrote a letter to the local paper in 1981.

"There is no indication to date, now 1981, that any such attempt to consider these recommendations has been undertaken," said Mr. Selden. "In fact, there are indications of a desire on the part of the current majority of borough council to discourage cooperation with the township despite a willingness on the part of the township committee to hold the current hearings on cable television in joint sessions, since they are facing the same issues for this single community. The borough council voted four to two against such mutual activities. The president of borough council is quoted as saying that 'the needs of the two municipalities are too different and the lines of questioning would be too diverse." [*Town Topics*, "Mailbox," January 7, 1981]

The report also had additional recommendations that would have proven helpful in encouraging closer collaboration. These too, made it no further than the report. The recommendations, however, are important, because they are relevant to the efforts of other towns looking to collaborate more closely and build rapport and trust with their neighboring communities. They are provided below with a notation of how each recommendation was disregarded by the future governing bodies in the decades afterward.

- *Appointments to boards and commissions should be based on talent not geography, i.e., not be limited to only borough or township residents respectively – appointments should be open to the most qualified members of the entire Princeton community.*

During my tenure in government, most advisory boards had continued to include only residents from the municipality in which the board was located unless it was a shared board or commission. For example, the township and borough continued to have separate traffic and transportation committees yet the issues facing each committee would certainly overlap and affect each other.

- *The two municipalities should adopt the same budget forms and procedures with the same accounting categories and classifications. For audits, a single auditor should be appointed for both municipalities.*

This never happened. Outside of the standardization of public budget documents, there were no coordinating budget procedures, accounting categories or classifications outside of already shared departments. The towns continued to use separate auditors.

- *Adopt a comprehensive joint purchasing program to include benefits, insurance, etc.*

The towns continued to purchase on their own and failed to collaborate on benefits or insurance purchasing.

- *Reassessment of all properties in both the borough and township should be conducted on an annual basis (i.e. prevents negative equalization effects upon consolidation).*

The reassessment recommendation was perhaps the most important forward-looking recommendation from the commission in light of the consolidation vote being rejected. The towns disregarded an annual reassessment or readjustment program, and even though reassessments would be performed together in future years, they would often occur decades apart resulting in some residents experience significant changes in their property taxes. In 2009/2010 the towns conducted a full reassessment of properties. Because of the 10-year time frame between the 2009 reassessment and the previous reassessment, many smaller homes experienced dramatic increases in property taxes, as their values grew at a much faster pace in 10 years versus the values of the larger, more expensive properties.

In other communities looking to consolidate, tax rate equalization is a crucial factor. Equalization of tax rates and divergent assessments could be a deal breaker for consolidation as one community may gain a significant short-term tax advantage over the other town resulting in an unbalanced benefit.

- *More extensive inter-municipal coordination between the borough and the township should be employed in planning for the acquisition and use of office space.*

The towns continued with their own plans for office space and municipal operations. The township built a new and expensive municipal building, and this was a key issue brought up by the borough anti-consolidation group during the 1996 referendum vote as it was in the planning stages at that time.

In addition, each public works department had its own facilities while both had a clear and present need for cold storage. Closer coordination prior to the 2011 consolidation referendum could have resulted in a single cold storage facility and lower capital costs for equipment that would have a longer lifespan with adequate protection from the elements.

- *Coordinate the purchase of major equipment to prevent redundancies and share/complement equipment with the other municipality.*

While some public works equipment would be shared from time to time, the towns generally purchased their own capital equipment for public works and police with very little coordination on major purchases. The only exception was for fire department equipment as that was a shared service between the two municipalities.

- *Keep accurate records of the extent of investment of one municipality in property held in title by the other municipality.*

Outside of real estate, this would become an important issue in future years especially in regard to the Princeton Sewer Operating Committee operations and investment of each town in sewer facilities. The towns failed to keep good records of sewer investments, a factor that proved contentious in future years.

- *When ordinances are adopted on the same subject, the format and verbiage should be made as similar as possible with respect to numbers and orders of sections, as well as in wording of the various provisions.*

This recommendation was rarely followed in future years. A major issue often discussed during the attempt to consolidate was the anticipated challenge of reconciliation of ordinances in a very short amount of time post consolidation. However, with the passage of the Local Option Municipal Consolidation Act in 2007, ordinances would have a longer timeframe for reconciliation, thus adding additional flexibility to the process.

- *The police departments coordinate on joint dispatch*

The towns were still talking about joint dispatch when I was first elected in 2006, 27 years after the concluding report. Only after the successful consolidation vote in 2011 would the towns begin to institute a joint dispatch. Throughout the years, separate dispatch and jurisdiction issues would be constant problems. This was illustrated in the case of the Fine Tower suicide, when a student jumped off the top floor of the Princeton University building Fine Tower (which straddles the township/borough line) and a township/borough police fight ensued over jurisdiction of the investigation.

- *The municipalities should engage a consultant and conduct departmental studies to find more effective and efficient ways of operating departments and deliver services more efficiently.*

That did happen, for example, in the case of Princeton Township – which hired a police consultant to take a closer look at finding efficiencies in the police department. However, the Princeton Township consultant never mandated sharing police services. The consultant did include a recommendation for a joint dispatch that was never implemented.

The commission's concluding report was a thoughtful document whose recommendations, for the most part, were never followed. The commission's final recommendation was that the planning board – already a joint entity – should work with the joint municipal operations committee to implement portions of these recommendations. This suggestion also was ignored.

Couples therapy failed miserably. With virtually none of the concluding report's suggestions implemented, the towns went their separate ways. The next year, in 1980, the Princeton Borough Council voted to raise taxes by 40 percent, prompting about 100 outraged voters to pack town hall in a protest that had no impact. A former borough councilman and leader of the consolidation effort in 1979, Bill Selden, noted: "We who worked on the consolidation committee anticipated that the borough taxes would rise faster than the township's." It was an I-told-you-so moment that only served to fan the flames of resentment and regret between the two towns.

Déjà vu – all over again, said Yogi Berra, offering a prescient comment relevant to the Princeton consolidation/collaboration efforts, whether those efforts were holistic or departmental. A decade later the towns again would consider uniting. Starting in 1990, Princeton Borough Councilman Mark Freda, who would later chair the Princeton Transition Task Force after the successful vote in 2011, helped broker a study for a single, shared service police department. That effort also ended without the sought-after result. The township police were concerned about the chain of command that would be rendered dysfunctional by operating with two separate governing bodies.

In 1991, the question of forming another study commission for full municipal consolidation was considered. At a meeting held by the League of Women Voters, many residents gathered to test the waters for revisiting consolidation again.

Former Princeton Township Mayor and 1979 Consolidation Commission Member Jay Bleiman quipped: "We are not trying to merge Egypt and Israel, just the borough and township. Maybe now that East and West Germany are merged, it will set an example for the two Princetons."[*Town Topics*, "Consolidation Study Probably Will Appear On November Ballots," February, 6, 1991]

The effort to put the question of studying consolidation on the referendum ballot in each town began with the formation of the Princeton Citizens Committee for The Study of Consolidation. Residents first approached the township and the borough governing bodies to pass an ordinance placing the question on the ballot. The township approved the ordinance and the borough failed to do so.

Unfazed, the committee then conducted a petition drive to obtain the required number of signatures to force the ballot question in the borough and the township. The Princeton Citizens Committee was successful in obtaining enough signatures enabling the referendum vote to move forward. The borough, however, would vote it down by 377 votes -- 1198 opposing the referendum and 821 in favor of it. To reiterate, this was a vote for just *studying* consolidation, not actually implementing consolidation.

A resident with anti-consolidation leanings declared in victory: "Consolidation is like a vampire. It rises from the grave and has to be returned every few years." [Town Topics, "Consolidation Vote: A Familiar Refrain: Wins in Township and Loses in Borough Again," November 6, 1991]

Thinking As One Town – Report of the Joint Consolidation Study Commission (June 30, 1996)

Four years later, however, consolidation reared its head again. In 1995, the voters in Princeton Borough and Township approved the formation of another study commission. Their report, entitled "Thinking As One Town," elaborated upon many of the same themes of the 1979 commission report. In recommending full consolidation, they provided the following summary themes (excerpts from the 1996 report):

- Giving voice to the whole community – *"Because most decisions made in the borough or township actually affect the lives of citizens in both municipalities, one Princeton will give all citizens a say in all of the decisions that affect their future, rather than in only part of these decisions."* The commission outlined several examples where joint decision making in a single community would be beneficial to the downtown (borough) business district and the more rural open spaces of the township.

- Identifying facilities needed by the whole community – *"One Princeton will be able to address a whole range of common community needs – including a well-designed senior center, active outdoor recreation fields, indoor winter recreation included in a community center, and a library that reflects the quality of the town which it is located. These common needs are much more difficult for two Princetons to agree upon and adequately fund."*

Agreeing to the size, scope and location of common facilities between two or more towns can be a daunting task. While the 1996 effort was unsuccessful at the voting booth, the concept and challenges of joint funding for joint facilities between two governments were important. Up until the 2011 vote, this was a major obstacle for the municipalities and many goals that had been discussed for decades simply never made it to the agenda between the governing bodies. The reconstruction of the towns' pool complex was a particularly daunting task between the two municipal governments and the recreation board – something that consolidation would have made much easier.

- Providing common facilities for police and town administration – *"One Princeton will be able to build common physical facilities for its administration and police at substantially less cost than the more than $11 million that the two municipalities are planning to spend on separate borough and township facilities (more than $15 million if the cost of servicing the resulting debt is added to it)."*

At the time of this discussion, the township was actively preparing to build a multi-million dollar municipal facility that it ended up building. When consolidation would later pass 15 years later, retooling that facility resulted in extra transition related costs that could have been saved if the towns came together earlier or shared space. However, the theme of common facilities did result in some unforeseen savings when the towns eventually did combine. In 2013, the newly consolidated Princeton relocated some departments to the old borough administration building, instead of constructing a newer building -- a project that would have gone forward, if the towns remained separate.

- Providing common facilities for public works - Both towns had separate public works facilities, and, as mentioned earlier in the analysis of the 1979 commission's concluding report, both towns needed a cold storage facility to house their equipment. In addition, a common facility would help to coordinate deployment and communication during emergencies.

- Achieving economies of scale with the Princeton Regional School District - The commission found opportunity in having a single government work with the school district to share facilities and leverage equipment and maintenance operations.

- Providing community-wide policing and public works - *"One Princeton would be able to consolidate its separate police and separate public works departments which account for three out of four dollars in the budgets of the two municipalities, maintaining effective service and eliminating uncertainties of service delivery along the invisible boundary between the borough and township."*

This crucial theme in the report would be proven after the successful consolidation in 2012, when the town responded to the crisis presented by Hurricane Sandy. The police department also would be able to reinstitute its safe neighborhoods community policing initiative and better serve the whole town.

- Dealing with Princeton's tax-exempt institutions – *"One Princeton will be more effective in dealing with its tax exempt institutions."*

In the case of the borough and township, having two governing bodies negotiate voluntary contributions or payments-in-lieu of taxes (PILOTs) was a difficult task. Furthermore, it was easy for elected officials to grandstand and use these negotiations to score political points but not necessarily results, especially with Princeton University. When the towns merged in 2013, the new town negotiated the highest voluntary contribution ever with Princeton University and did so with a long-term agreement providing predictability in future budget years.

- Dealing with external development pressures – *"One Princeton will be more effective in dealing with the intense pressures that the community faces from development in central New Jersey and the Boston to Washington corridor."*

The commission in 1996 recognized that having a single town advocating forcefully for its interests coupled with a single town planning for its collective future on issues such as traffic and zoning is a benefit of consolidation that often fails to be discussed.

From a financial perspective, the commission estimated budget savings of $500,000 to $1.4 million in annual savings depending on the staff cuts that were made by the new governing body. This was coupled with an analysis of the joint departments (a.k.a. shared services) of the two towns that showed smaller budget increases during the past 25 years than the four departments that remained separate. In addition, the towns' combined police departments spent more on police services than most other New

Jersey towns of similar size. [*The Times of Trenton*, "One Princeton or Two?," September 10, 1995]

In 1996, the tax rates and debt burdens for both towns were similar this time too. The 1965 commission reported that even though consolidation was feasible, the divergent tax rates made consolidation prohibitive at the time because it would provide an unequal benefit to one town over the other. This time, however, the fiscal stars were lining up.

With the commission recommending consolidation, the question was again put to the voters. Just as in 1979, a pro-consolidation group focused on advertisements in the local paper and letters-to-the-editor to promote their viewpoints and argue their case. Their ads focused on the broad, strategic goals of consolidation.

The Case FOR Consolidation:

Five More Reasons to Vote for One Princeton

☑ **To deliver better municipal services at less cost**
One Community, more efficient and effective

☑ **To meet common challenges with one voice,** renovating our library, acquiring new recreation sites, joining together to preserve our historic community
One Community, united

☑ **To strengthen our voice in the region,** dealing as one with State and County, the surrounding towns, and the non-profit organizations that dominate our local economy
One Community, stronger

☑ **To protect everyone's downtown and open space**
One Community, pulling together

☑ **To take advantage of financial equilibrium,** at a time when the municipal tax rates and debt burdens of the Borough and Township are in balance
One Community, in balance

P.O. Box 1595, Princeton, NJ 08542
(609) 252-1173

Paid for by One Princeton, Herb Gurk, Treasurer

1996 One Princeton Pro-Consolidation Ad

Preserve Our Historic Borough (POHB) was the main anti-consolidation group and they took a hard line against consolidation – one that exceeded the aggressiveness in community ads compared to the prior anti-consolidation effort of 1979.

One familiar argument from the anti-consolidation side was that consolidation would result in bigger government. It is a hard argument to make when the whole concept of consolidation is to do more with less – fewer elected officials and fewer duplicative staffers. Yet, the anti-consolidation group ran with it, distributing this controversial flyer ahead of the vote in 1996.

HISTORY SHOWS THAT ONCE YOU START CONSOLIDATING,
IT'S HARD TO STOP

THE MORE POWER YOU HAVE,
THE MORE POWER YOU WANT.

TODAY IT'S PRINCETON BORO AND PRINCETON TOWNSHIP.
TOMORROW IT'S PRINCETON JUNCTION.
NEXT THURSDAY IT MIGHT BE THE WINDSORS.
AND NEXT YEAR IT MIGHT BE PITTSBURG.

BIG BROTHER ALWAYS HAS HIS REASONS,
AND BIG BROTHER IS NEVER SATISFIED.

DON'T LET BIG BROTHER GET ANY BIGGER

VOTE **NO** ON CONSOLIDATION !

paid for by POHB, 18 Cleveland Lane, Princeton, NJ

1996 POHB Flyer

Even more disturbing in the flyer was that it showed ruthless former dictators and attempted to equate Princeton's consolidation attempt to their attempts at world domination.

The letters-to-the-editor were no more civil. Resident and anti-consolidation advocate, Orren Jack Turner, responded to Borough Councilman Roger Martindell's letter comparing consolidation to a marriage. Mr. Turner declared: "So, today, while the 'bride' is being dragged down the aisle, kicking and screaming 'no,' the groomsmen suavely chat up the press on the church steps about living happily ever after. If I weren't constrained to maintain civility in this matter, I would term the whole affair 'date rape.' Doesn't 'no' mean 'no' anymore, except on college campuses?" [*Town Topics*, Letter To The Editor, July 31, 1996]

This commission recommended consolidation. It ultimately failed in Princeton Borough. This time by a wider margin:1878 voting against and 1518 voting in favor. The township voted for consolidation by a more than two to one margin: 4350 for to 1622 against.

The 1996 referendum failure dealt what many thought could have been the fatal blow to consolidation of the two Princetons. It also left a great deal of animosity between the borough and the township that would take more than a decade to heal. Township residents and committee members discussed potentially changing the cost sharing arrangements on the joint, shared departments to make them more equitable – in their estimation. In 2007, the passage of the Local Option Municipal Consolidation Act and two willing governing bodies brought the issue to the forefront again.

Old Guard

"It's hard to imagine anything could be more transparent than the charade we've just witnessed. But stay tuned we've surely not seen the last of two-faced politics in this one-party town."

– ***The Princeton Packet*** "Editorial," March 31, 2006

Princeton's politics were changing. Influenced by the ripple currents of Howard Dean's 2004 run for the presidency, many Princeton residents were invigorated and ready to become involved locally on a grassroots level. The local Democratic club known as the Princeton Community Democratic Organization (PCDO), however, tended to be off-putting to newcomers. It was tough for an outsider to break through the wall of the Democratic Party Old Guard – or the incumbent elected officials who also dominated the political landscape.

That was about to change. Sometimes one is in the wrong place at the wrong time, or in my case the right place at the right time. In the fall of 2005, I became more involved with the PCDO. I became a member, attended membership meetings and events, and I met Jenny Crumiller, a local, grassroots activist, who was also becoming more involved. She and her group of Democratic friends cut their teeth on many historic New Jersey campaigns, but locally they had gained some notoriety for their opposition to the hospital expansion in town. That also gained them some infamous credentials with the current governing body – the body that was indirectly in the control of the PCDO.

In 2006, Jenny decided to run for president of the PCDO. She had a clear vision, and most of all, wanted to open the organization up to more members and increase transparency in the organization. This was important because the PCDO was the main vehicle for electing people to office in Princeton Borough and Princeton Township. Republicans had very little chance locally. A Democrat wanting to run for office had to go through the endorsement process of the PCDO. The establishment officials in Princeton Township and Princeton Borough were unenthusiastic about welcoming Jenny to become the president of the PCDO. Welcoming new people into the party's positions of power was seen as a threat. In this case, the existing elected officials had sought someone to challenge her, but in the end Jenny prevailed convincingly.

Ultimately, Jenny's victory brought more people into the PCDO and that was a positive development for the organization and for the towns.

A few months later, something would happen that led to my involvement on the local political scene. A five member governing body called a township committee - with each committeeperson elected to a three-year term - governed Princeton Township. The five committee members then selected a mayor and deputy mayor for annual terms. In March, one of the members of the committee, Democrat Bill Hearon, announced that he was resigning and would not finish his term. The PCDO swung into action to help find a replacement to be appointed and serve for the remainder of his term.

The PCDO announced a call for candidates to come forward. The township governing body clearly favored the outgoing PCDO president, Scott Carver, and most thought that he would be endorsed by the PCDO membership to fill the vacant committee slot. However, the new leadership at the PCDO insisted on an open call for candidates. I decided that, while I probably wouldn't win this time around, it would be good for me to get my name out there. As a result, I put my name forward. Five candidates including myself appeared at a candidates' night where we each gave a several minute speech and then answered questions from the audience afterwards.

In my presentation, I highlighted my interest in starting a dialogue with Princeton Borough. The last failed consolidation attempt in

1996 left the two governing bodies constantly bickering. Lack of communication between the two towns was at an all-time low.

To that end, I also felt that consolidation should be a key issue for the towns as it presented an opportunity to save money and make our towns' services more effective. The governing bodies seemed focused on minutiae when there were clearly large structural improvements, like consolidation, that could make a real impact. I was willing to dedicate myself to furthering that cause and I wanted to make it clear to the membership.

All the candidates answered a myriad of questions on topics ranging from budgets to deer control. At the end, members voted for their preferred candidate by secret ballot. In order to get the club's endorsement, a candidate needed to secure 60 percent of the vote. With five candidates, that would be difficult, but even a majority of votes would position a candidate well for the next evening's Municipal Democratic Committee – giving him or her a clear advantage.

While votes were being counted, I waited in the back of the room with a neighbor who had come to the meeting with me. Before I knew it, the head ballot counter was making the announcement that I won the most votes for the evening – much to my surprise – and apparently the surprise of several of the party insiders. As I was leaving the meeting, one member of township committee mentioned that perhaps I could get appointed to a municipal board or commission at the end of this process. This was her way of clearly indicating to me that my candidacy failed to win her approval.

The next evening I spoke in front of the Municipal Democratic Committee and earned its full endorsement, thus all but ensuring my appointment to the now vacant seat. Little did I know that the appointment was no sure thing.

It was in March of 2006 when I entered the township hall to be appointed to the vacant committee seat. Township hall was a relatively new building with a large meeting room and in the front of the room was a dais where the township committee would sit. The press was there to cover my appointment and the Municipal Democratic Committee chair sat behind me as we waited for the committee to get to the appointment. A reporter leaned over and asked me if I had a moment to talk to him in the hallway. I followed him out, and he asked me how I felt about serving on the committee, what I wanted to accomplish, etc. Suddenly, the township administrator came out into the hallway and said "we're ready for you now." I returned to my seat to see the evening unfold.

Just as the committee was getting to the appointment on the agenda, the resigning township committee member, Bill Hearon, whom I was replacing, took the microphone on the dais. He announced that he was going to rescind his resignation and essentially eliminated my appointment to the committee. The Princeton Packet "Editorial," March 31, 2006, summed it up:

"Township Committeeman Bill Hearon decides to step down just a few months before his three-year term is scheduled to end. He is doing so, he says, because he urgently needs to devote more time to his business, but everybody knows that's not the real reason. The real reason is to allow his colleagues to choose his successor, thus giving a fellow Democrat the advantage of incumbency in the upcoming election.

Everybody knows, though no one will say so, that the other four members of the township committee would like Mr. Hearon's successor to be Scott Carver, the former president of the Princeton Community Democratic Organization. But Mr. Carver fails to win the endorsement of the PCDO, whose leadership has recently changed hands and direction. Everybody knows, though no one will say so, that the party has split into two camps: one loyal to Jenny Crumiller, the new PCDO president, the other allied with the establishment, represented by, among others, the sitting members of the township committee.

What everyone knows, but no one will say, is that Mr. Hearon's change of heart was occasioned less by his own misgivings about the process of choosing his successor than by his colleagues' disappointment in the outcome of that process. They didn't want to appoint Mr. Goerner, but they couldn't very well appoint Mr. Carver, after he had removed his name from consideration. So Mr. Hearon decided to stay on and now everyone can claim, though no one actually believes, that they feel so much more comfortable seeing their party's candidate chosen through an open, transparent process.

It's hard to imagine anything could be more transparent than the charade we've just witnessed. But stay tuned we've surely not seen the last of two-faced politics in this one-party town." The Princeton Packet, Editorial, March 31, 2006

As a result of the meeting, Scott Carver decided to get back in the race and run against me in the June primary. The campaign went into full swing. I had a chance to meet with many major stakeholders in the community, identified likely voters and went door-to-door, and also held a series of open meetings in virtually all the neighborhoods in Princeton.

In the end, it paid off. I won the primary with 70 percent of the vote. The effort of campaigning allowed me to forge relationships with many Democrats and elected officials in the borough and Mercer County. It was a bumpy road to office, but now it was time to get to work.

Star-crossed Lovers

"The consolidation story of Princeton is like the tragic story of two star-crossed lovers meeting passionately almost once a decade only to veer off course when it came time to negotiate the prenuptials."

– Chad Goerner, "Princeton Consolidation is Inevitable," The Princeton Packet, October 2007

In my first full year in office, change was in the air. Initially, it was challenging to work with my governing body colleagues who didn't really want me as a colleague. However, as time went on, we were able to work together effectively. Proof of that fact was when the committee agreed to approve two of my campaign promises: an open application process for board and commissions and the establishment of a citizens' finance advisory commission. Next up was to continue to foster relations with Princeton Borough and begin the dialogue of consolidation.

At the same time, the NJ State Legislature acted to make the conversation about consolidation even easier. Proposed legislation established the Local Unit Alignment, Reorganization and Consolidation Commission (LUARCC). Its mission would be to recommend consolidation to certain towns. In the original bill, if the towns voted consolidation down in referendum, the municipalities would lose state aid. These provisions would later be removed from the legislation leaving LUARCC gutted and pretty much powerless. Before the bill was changed, however, it was clear that change would be coming whether we liked it or not. Therefore, I proposed that it would be better if we controlled our own destiny and studied consolidation at the local level, as opposed to having the state dictate what the towns had to do. In a series of op/eds beginning in October of 2007, I –

ignoring the naysayers – opened up the Pandora's box of consolidation dialogue.

I saw two main drivers behind the consolidation movement in 2007. First, initiating a dialogue with Princeton Borough Council, which may sound rudimentary and obvious, was so important because it was not happening when I first came into office. Princeton Township and Princeton Borough – behaving like many towns across the state – defended the sanctity of their home rule by placing the blame on the other town when they had to make difficult decisions. This attitude was no different in 2007. That began to change subtly, as members of borough council and I made concerted efforts to open the lines of communication.

We did what any two people would do when attempting to build a relationship – find common ground. We started in one area by finding common ground on traffic and transportation. The towns are transected by state highway 206 and had spent many years attempting to combat heavy truck traffic to no avail by promoting alternative routes and targeted enforcement. The state, however, got the two communities to communicate by sponsoring a traffic-calming study forcing the towns to work together. Even though it never came to fruition (the state lacked further funding and commitment), it did serve to build rapport between the two towns.

The second driver of getting consolidation going was the passage of the New Jersey Local Option Municipal Consolidation Act in mid-2007. This act was modeled after the last unsuccessful effort of consolidation in the Princetons in 1996.Its goal was to provide flexibility to the consolidation process. It had some promising provisions. The op/ed I wrote in the fall of 2007 aimed to provide the community with some insight into how Princeton could use this new law to finally make consolidation successful.

To get the process moving, the governing bodies could simply apply to the Local Finance Board in the Division of Community Affairs to establish a consolidation commission rather than having the question placed on the ballot. That not only would expedite the process, but also would permit a more flexible timetable than under the alternative Municipal Consolidation Act. The commission would be able to engage the community in a grassroots effort to forge consensus.

If the towns would form a commission, they would benefit from the true flexibility in the enhanced Municipal Consolidation Act providing additional opportunities for consolidation. This included the following:

· Advisory Planning Districts – The law allowed the creation of districts consisting of residents who would advise the planning board and newly unified zoning board of adjustment on applications and master plan changes affecting areas that they live in. The aim here was to preserve neighborhood character – often an initial objection to consolidation in Princeton (the borough especially).

· Maintaining Local Ordinances – The new law allowed the "continued use of boundary lines of any or all of the former municipalities to continue local ordinances that existed prior to consolidation that the governing body deems necessary and appropriate." For example, ordinances in the township could still exist where one may not be present in the borough or vice-versa provided that the combined municipality deems them necessary and reviews them periodically (every five years).

· Apportionment of Debt – The act allowed apportionment of debt, if an analysis of the debt of each municipality proves to be an obstacle due to disproportion. Thus, taxpayers could continue to be responsible for their own pre-consolidation debts. This provision was a key change from earlier laws and provided flexibility that could become important in a consolidation effort. If one town had a higher debt burden than the other, it could prevent the two towns from consolidating, since one town would gain a disproportional benefit.

· Service Districts – If a certain service (i.e. trash collection, leaf and brush collection) were provided in one municipality but not another, and it is the will of the municipality to continue it in that manner, service districts could be established to maintain the same level or version of service.

· Phased-In Consolidation – The revision to the act allowed for a phased-in consolidation that could perhaps allow towns to first consolidate the governing bodies and phase-in more sensitive departments over a specific time-frame to ensure the same quality level of service to the towns' residents.

The legislation also provided a credit to a municipality that had a negative effect resulting from the equalization of tax rates at the time of consolidation. The credit would offset the impact of equalization on the resident's property tax until they sold the home. Unfortunately, this credit was never funded by the legislature. Even though it could have eliminated one of the major obstacles of consolidation towns were unable to take advantage of this provision.

Over the course of the following year, I worked with several members of borough council and discussed consolidation, particularly why it would make sense to form a commission to study it. Some members were enthusiastic about the prospect of looking at consolidation armed with a more flexible piece of legislation to aid the effort. I teamed up with a former committeewoman in the township, Roz Denard, and two councilmembers from Princeton Borough, Wendy Benchley and Barbara Trelstad, to write an op/ed in support of a consolidation study - the first borough/township public support for consolidation.

The following two columns describe the consolidation case succinctly yet comprehensively – and started the towns on another lap of the consolidation marathon.

GUEST OPINION: "The case for Princeton consolidation," **Chad Goerner, Roz Denard, Wendy Benchley, Barbara Trelstad**, [*The Princeton Packet*, April 2, 2009]

The 1996 report of the Consolidation Study Commission's "Thinking as One Town," outlined a prescient concern if the township and the borough remained separate municipalities: "We believe that two municipalities will be less able to agree upon and fund a range of community-wide needs."

That moment has all but arrived. Princeton Township and Princeton Borough are quite unique in that we have a large number of joint commissions all of which are funded jointly by both municipalities. When Princeton Borough (approximately 1.8 square miles) is faced with a finite ratable base and hemmed in by a large tax-exempt entity, it is only inevitable that in time its budget needs outgrow its ability to fund them without either service cuts or significant increases in property taxes.

This unfortunate circumstance coupled with the current economic environment can cause Princeton Borough to reduce or eliminate their funding for certain joint services. When this happens, the Township is then forced to eliminate or significantly scale back on the service too as they will not be able to fund the full cost on their own. The end result becomes an elimination or reduction of services for both Borough and Township residents.

We all have served or are currently serving on our respective governing bodies. We both feel that whether one resides in the township or the borough, what makes Princeton the place we call home are a vibrant and successful central business district and our wonderful open space. We both see our community as truly one town and see a way forward: full municipal consolidation. While consolidation will never be the answer to all the issues facing our communities, it has the potential to:

• Deliver services more cost-effectively and efficiently – One police department, one public works department and one administration will result in cost savings and reduced overlap.

Eliminating joint commissions will save time in executing service delivery.

• Have our governing bodies focus on governing again – What percentage of time has minutiae occupied the governing bodies' agendas, while other, more important issues were moved to the background? A consolidated government will allow us to truly govern as one community and focus on long-term vision.

• Plan our future as one town – There is no question that the Central Business District of Princeton Borough remains a core trait of our community identity and it is vital to both municipalities. As we develop bike routes and sidewalks in the township to encourage flow to the downtown, the pathways should go beyond the borough line. Mass transit services should be considered holistically and be integrated within both municipalities. When township officials are considering housing options for its 55 and older population, they should be able to look at real opportunities closer to the town center where there is better access to transportation and volunteer activities. If we are one town, we can better integrate our planning.

• Engage Princeton University as One Town – As stated in the 1996 Study "Consolidation would create a stronger municipality to deal strategically with its tax-exempt institutions while it eliminated the red tape created by two sets of administrative processes." Working with the university as one municipality will allow us to better prioritize our concerns and needs for the betterment of the entire community.

• Better Application of State Aid – A municipality of 30,000 residents will command more attention than two separate municipalities whose identities are often confused by state employees outside of Mercer County. Grants and assistance will flow to one municipality instead of two where they will then be implemented to the benefit of the entire municipality instead of just one without the cooperation or input of the other.

We recognize that this will not be an easy task and that history has proved consolidation difficult. If we are to engage in this process again we must remain sensitive to the concerns raised by residents of both municipalities. We must encourage discussion and dialogue in order to make the effort successful.

As you may know, the state has passed a Local Option Consolidation Act that was modeled on the prior consolidation failures in the Princetons. Our next article will address some of the questions and concerns that we have heard from our constituents in regard to municipal consolidation and how the new Local Option Consolidation Act could alleviate some of these concerns.

On April 27, the governing bodies have agreed to hold a joint public meeting on the consolidation of services and municipal consolidation. The meeting will be held at 7:00PM at the Princeton Township Hall, 400 Witherspoon Street. We encourage you to attend this important meeting.

—Chad Goerner, Deputy Mayor, Princeton Township

—Roz Denard, former Committeewoman, Princeton Township

—Barbara Trelstad, Councilwoman, Princeton Borough

—Wendy Benchley, former Councilwoman, Princeton Borough

Shortly after the publication of this op/ed re-introducing consolidation and the expanded flexibilities under the new Local Option law, we put together a question and answer op/ed in an effort to be proactive in addressing any lingering concerns that might prevent a study from getting off the ground. Because of Princetons' history with consolidation, we wanted to get out in front of the inevitable concerns and anti-consolidation interests.

GUEST OPINION: "A Way Forward On Princeton Consolidation," **Chad Goerner, Barbara Trelstad, Wendy Benchley,** [The Princeton Packet, April 23, 2009]

The Local Option Municipal Consolidation Act that was passed in 2007 provides additional flexibility to the consolidation process and was created as a direct result of the failure of the last consolidation study in the Princetons. We have gathered some of the concerns and questions that residents have posed to us on consolidation and address how a consolidation study under the local option could address them.

We don't want to lose neighborhood character or the vibrancy of the central business district. How do we make sure that this doesn't happen in a consolidated municipality?

A new feature of the local option provides for "Advisory Planning Districts." Advisory Planning Districts can be established to allow specific areas of town that are sensitive to new development or change with a direct ability to provide input on any new development affecting their district or any master plan changes. The regional planning board in a public forum must address any concerns raised by an advisory planning district. Many times when an application comes before the planning board, it is sometimes difficult for neighbors to coordinate their concerns effectively. This innovative structure would enable the newly consolidated municipality to still have specific planning districts that look to preserve the character and uniqueness of either the central business district or neighborhoods.

One of the biggest potential threats to the downtown central business district could be the borough's ratable base. At 1.8 square miles, the borough has a finite base and may make revenue decisions that could ultimately harm the character of the downtown. An active vibrant central business district is vital for the sustainability of the community. Borough and township residents value the current variety of stores in the central business district for their uniqueness.

Change to building height and character could be a greater potential threat in the years ahead as revenue options become more and more limited and the only way to build is up. This has been discussed by the borough governing body in the past and could very well come to the forefront in future revenue related discussions.

How does each municipality retain its voice in the new government?

What we would hope from this process is that we move away from this "us versus them" mentality and understand that the decisions that each municipality makes affect the other. We are already one area with housing built around a central business district and children attending a unified school system. What we need to do is take a 30,000-foot view of what is really happening around us. Township residents have as much vested interest in the vitality of the downtown as borough residents.

Do we really need 12 elected officials to govern a population of 30,000? Do we really need two police departments and two administrations? Do we really need two municipal building complexes? Is this really the most effective and efficient way for us to deliver services to our residents?

The reality is that we are all in this together as one community yet we cannot efficiently act as one with our current structure. The consolidation study would evaluate the best form of government for the new single municipality. Depending on the form of government, certain representation safeguards would ensure that current borough or township residents would have a continued voice in government. Some towns use a combination of wards and governing members "at-large." This would allow for specific representation of residents in specific areas of town and still allow for broad, at-large representation—a better system than currently in place. For example, Morristown consists of a 7 member governing body: three members at-large representing the entire town and four members representing each of the town's four wards. This, of course, is just an example but it is an important one in emphasizing that the governing body in a consolidated municipality would certainly be able to represent the interests of different areas of town based on a customized government structure.

As mentioned earlier, advisory planning districts also provide an additional voice for residents in specific neighborhoods. This is an additional opportunity to protect the voice of our neighborhoods and districts for both current township and borough residents.

Ordinances may be different in the township than they are in the borough (i.e. Flood Control Ordinance, Pet Leash Ordinance, etc.) and it may prove difficult to reconcile them. What do we do?

Under the local option, existing ordinances can remain under the borders of the previous municipality. Again, this flexibility is available to help a consolidated municipality move forward without getting stuck on the smaller issues that can take some time to resolve. A systematic ordinance-by-ordinance review could be put in place at the outset to gradually consolidate ordinances over a period of time. Furthermore, the act requires that the new governing body must review any ordinances that remain under the borders of the previous municipality every five years to see if they are still necessary and relevant.

I don't want to be responsible for the debt of the other municipality.

The local option provides for the apportionment of debt so that each municipality is responsible for their own debt pre-consolidation and new debt incurred by the consolidated municipality is then shared equally.

Will consolidation save costs in delivering services?

One main goal of consolidation is to eliminate overlap and streamline the delivery of services to residents. This should certainly result in significant cost savings for the municipality. The Buracker report estimated that the consolidation of the police alone would generate significant annual savings. Add to that overlap in administration, engineering, public works, construction, etc. and those savings should increase.

Please join us on Monday, April 27, 7 p.m. at Township Hall (400 Witherspoon Street) to learn more about municipal consolidation.

EDITOR'S NOTE: This opinion piece was submitted by Princeton Township Deputy Mayor Chad Goerner, Princeton Borough Council member Barbara Trelstad and former Borough Council member Wendy Benchley.

With these public statements, we began to lay the groundwork for a formal proposal to study consolidation. It had the feeling of a Sisyphean task. Each failed effort in the Princetons brought long lasting animosity or just intensified a numb indifference. Many citizens were long-time residents with institutional memories of multiple failed efforts. Some were simply pessimistic that it would have a chance.

Gathering input from members of both governing bodies, I began working on a proposal for the governing bodies to consider.

Not the C-Word Again!

"I think we can go forward with the next two or three steps without throwing the c-word in front of everybody and getting an uproar and having everybody taking sides."

– **Princeton Borough Councilman David Goldfarb** "Consensus Forms For Consolidation Study," *The Princeton Packet*, April 28, 2009

In order for the municipalities to consider consolidation after a series of failed attempts, this time had to be different. We had to have a clearly defined process and timeline. We also had to correct the issues that helped contribute to past failures. In part, we were aided by the more flexible NJ Local Option Municipal Consolidation Act and the wisdom of decades of failed attempts that exposed some consistent shortcomings.

All the prior commissions were either appointed or elected citizen commissioners. The issue with that is that the elected commissioners already had a perceived inherent bias and it was easier for the opposition to discredit their analysis. Furthermore, with no elected officials on the commission, it was easy for those officials to undermine the commission's work because they weren't part of the process. That had to change.

In the proposal to the governing bodies, I contemplated having an elected official and municipal staff commission, but was convinced by some allies on borough council that citizen representation would be important and help drive the workload that was going to be required. In the proposal, we settled on a commission structure comprising two elected officials from each municipality (appointed by the mayor with approval from the governing body), three citizen representatives from each municipality (appointed by the mayor with governing body approval and an open, public call for applications), each town's administrator (non-voting), and a representative that would be assigned from the New Jersey Department of Community Affairs (non-voting).

Another requirement outlined in the proposal was the use of an independent consultant. Previous attempts failed to utilize a dedicated, independent consultant who could present objective analysis to the community. The anti-consolidation group would question all analysis unless there were an independent third party. The first order of business for the commission would be to issue a request-for-proposal to select a consultant.

The proposal that I originally drafted for consideration was to study consolidation only. However, it became clear that there were several members of borough council that were more favorable to a shared service police force or public works department. It was important to have a unanimous vote as it would present symbolic faith in the process. Thus, the proposal was amended to include a study of shared services (police and public works) and full municipal consolidation.

The night that the governing bodies would review the proposal and resolution to form a commission was still contentious. Several members of borough council wanted to change wording to avoid, in their opinion, a positive view of consolidation. One member, David Goldfarb, unenthusiastic about consolidation, offered a cautionary tone as he recollected the last effort to consolidate in 1996.

"I thought the outcome was good for the community. I thought the process was very damaging to the relationship of the township and borough," Councilman Goldfarb said, as reported in _The Princeton Packet_. "I offer that as a word of caution because we have made some progress in restoring the relationship. Be careful what you wish for." [_The Princeton Packet_, "Borough, Township Authorize Consolidation Study," October 29, 2009]

The Princeton Packet labeled me unabashedly "one of the biggest proponents of the current effort to revisit the issue of full consolidation." While I made it clear that I was proud of the relationship that we had developed with the borough, I talked about the need to remove emotions from the initial stages of the process by using an independent consultant to do the number crunching and data analysis.

As we made the slight modifications to the resolution and grant application, we also heard from the public and many came out in support of the commission, although there were some detractors who did not think that revisiting an issue that had been voted down so many times made sense. Still, the governing bodies pushed forward, finally adopting the resolution and grant application with a unanimous vote.

"Unanimous; that has to be a first for the township and borough," Borough Mayor Mildred Trotman said and with that we began the process of forming a commission under the new Local Option Municipal Consolidation Act. [*The Princeton Packet*, "Borough, Township Authorize Consolidation Study," October 29, 2009]

Joint Shared Services and Consolidation Commission – Project Timeline Leading to the Voter Referendum [source: www.cgr.org/princeton/princetonprocessflowchart.pdf]

October 2009 – Both governing bodies approve the resolution to form a joint commission and approve an application to the New Jersey Local Finance Board.

December 2009 – Local Finance Board approves application to create the joint study commission.

June 2010 – The township and borough make appointments to the study commission.

September 2010 – The commission issues a RFP for consultant and selects the Center for Governmental Research (CGR).

October 2010 – The commission holds its first community-wide public forum.

January 2011 – Baseline analysis of current operations and finances is completed. The Baseline Report is completed.

February 2011 – The commission holds its second community-wide public forum to present the Baseline Report.

May 2011 – The commission and CGR complete analysis of options for consolidation and shared services. The Options Report is completed and presented to the public in another community-wide forum.

June/July 2011 – The commission issues their final recommendation to consolidate.

August 2011 – The governing bodies vote to put a referendum to consolidate on the ballot.

November 2011 – Voters approve consolidation by wide margins in both municipalities.

The Dream Team Mediators

"We have a fabulous opportunity in front of us in Princeton. An opportunity to be stronger, be more unified, be more efficient and to be a more harmonious community."

– **Joint Shared Services and Consolidation Commission Chair Anton Lahnston** – The Princeton Packet, June 2, 2011

Now that we had a proposal with an outline of how to proceed, it was time to form a commission. The commission would be called the Joint Shared Services and Consolidation Commission (JSSCC) and would consist of two elected officials from each municipality, three citizen representatives from each municipality, each town's administrator (non-voting) and a liaison from the New Jersey Department of Community Affairs (non-voting).

Both towns looked to seat their commissioners through an open call for applications, and we received dozens of applications from interested citizens. In the township, we aimed to include members that had backgrounds in finance, government, law, and public relations. Bernie Miller (mayor and then committeeman during the two-year consolidation study process) and I (also as deputy mayor and then mayor) were the elected official members for the township and Mayor Mildred Trotman and past anti-consolidation advocate Councilmember David Goldfarb were the elected officials representing the borough. (See appendix for complete list of commission members.)

While I mentioned my dismay about having Mr. Goldfarb on the committee, Mayor Trotman was insistent about including him in the process and responding to his comments as soon as he brought them up. She wanted him to be part of the process, rather than a critic of the process from afar. The next step for us was to find a chair – a citizen representative who could handle the delicate balancing that would be required both with the public and with the citizen and elected officials from both towns.

One of the borough representatives, Anton Lahnston, I knew to be a fair and firm leader who served with me on the town's joint bike committee. Prior to consolidation even though the towns were integrally connected, the municipalities had separate planning units for bike routes and sidewalks – a situation that caused many problems. Working with Anton, we created a Joint Bike and Pedestrian Committee – a forerunner of the consolidation discussion. He exhibited all the right skills to make an excellent chair of the commission.

I approached Mildred before our first meeting and asked her about Anton. To my delight, she also was going to recommend that he be the chair. So, we agreed that when it came time to nominate a chair we would nominate Anton. When he came into the room that evening, Mildred went up to him and said "just say yes, Anton." He looked perplexed and was unsure what was happening, but once the call for nominations went out he knew that he was going to be nominated for chair. He graciously accepted.

The position for the next several years would be a tremendous amount of work for little gratitude and a lot of aggravation. Anton approached the job with the professionalism of a major corporate CEO. He never lost sight of the ultimate goal of having the commission reach a conclusion – whether it was to recommend police and/or public works shared services, full consolidation, or nothing at all.

With the proposal serving as a guideline for the commission, the first and a most essential task was to find a suitable third-party consultant. In past consolidation efforts, the lack of an independent third-party left commissions without in-depth, independently verified data. The commissions thus were vulnerable to accusations of bias, thereby discrediting their work with some of the voters. While we had great financial and legal talent in the Princeton community, we needed the objective, independent analysis as the only way to ensure that the data would be untarnished by suspicions of bias.

In late 2010, the commission designed a request for proposal and conducted interviews with several finalists. The members ultimately selected the Center for Governmental Research (CGR) as the consultant to the commission. CGR's past involvement in a successful consolidation in New York State was of interest to some commissioners who were seeking a concrete example of consolidation, because there had been no successful, large-scale consolidations in the state of New Jersey in over a century.

CGR's process outlined several key report milestones that would serve to guide the commission in its work, as well as to inform the public and allow ample public input along the way. With the release of each report on the timeline, CGR and the commission would hold a joint public meeting to present the report, take feedback and answer questions with residents.

Baseline Report

The first step was developing a baseline report – essentially taking a snapshot of the municipal operations in each municipality. A crucial part of the process, this involved documenting debt levels, asset inventory, staffing and service delivery in each department and all necessary budget data. It helped all residents understand where each town stood from a fiscal standpoint, while simultaneously detailing critical information about the types of services provided in each town.

Common Category Expenditures	Township	Borough	Combined	
	---------- Dollars in Millions ----------			
Debt Service	$6.138	$3.831	$9.970	
Police	$3.779	$3.532	$7.312	
Stonybrook Regional Sewerage Authority	$2.260	$2.034	$4.294	
Insurance - Employee Group	$1.960	$2.192	$4.152	
Reserve for Uncollected Taxes	$2.534	$0.715	$3.249	
Street/Road Repair and Maintenance	$1.380	$0.678	$2.058	
Admin, Council and Clerk	$0.963	$0.741	$1.704	
Police and Fire Retirement System	$0.775	$0.738	$1.514	
Engineering	$0.812	$0.293	$1.104	
Construction Code	$0.722	$0.361	$1.082	*
Public Employees Retirement System	$0.533	$0.504	$1.037	
Affordable Housing (incl Dedicated Funds	$0.825	$0.111	$0.936	
Social Security	$0.400	$0.459	$0.859	
911/Dispatch	$0.416	$0.420	$0.835	
Buildings and Grounds	$0.285	$0.544	$0.829	
Fire Hydrant Service	$0.525	$0.143	$0.668	
Legal	$0.429	$0.196	$0.625	
Insurance - Liability	$0.257	$0.303	$0.560	
Financial Administration	$0.357	$0.193	$0.550	
Vehicle Maintenance/Mechanics	$0.299	$0.210	$0.509	
Municipal Court	$0.152	$0.336	$0.488	
Insurance - Workers Compensation	$0.189	$0.254	$0.443	
Fire Prevention	$0.100	$0.298	$0.398	
Electricity	$0.215	$0.120	$0.335	
Gas and Fuel Oil	$0.224	$0.080	$0.304	
Tax Collection	$0.161	$0.102	$0.263	
Street Lighting	$0.138	$0.118	$0.256	
Tax Assessment	$0.152	$0.046	$0.198	
Shade Tree Commission	$0.067	$0.126	$0.194	
Emergency Authorizations	$0.110	$0.061	$0.171	
Telephone	$0.050	$0.073	$0.123	
Municipal Prosecutor	$0.039	$0.037	$0.076	
Audit Services	$0.033	$0.035	$0.068	
Public Defender	$0.023	$0.037	$0.060	
Condominium Community Costs	$0.030	$0.008	$0.038	
Water	$0.013	$0.008	$0.021	
Elections	$0.008	$0.009	$0.018	
Emergency Management	$0.002	$0.009	$0.011	
Total	**$27.355**	**$19.956**	**$47.311**	

* Construction costs (and revenues) in the Township are "dedicated by rider" and thus do not appear in the general budget

Example of Baseline Report's expenditure comparison overview, CGR 2011

The police departments in each municipality generated specific interest and scrutiny for two reasons: 1) The departments were a potential shared service, if consolidation were not recommended; and 2) public safety services were the major cost centers for each town. The borough's police department had a budget of $3.5 million and the township's came in at $3.8 million. In addition, the towns also managed their own separate dispatch centers totaling a combined $800,000.

The baseline report and community presentation helped outline each department and gauge interest among the residents about which services were important, what residents would like to see improved, and where we could potentially save money.

Options Report

The commission, working with CGR, then developed an options report. This report provided different strategies for restructuring each municipal department under a single governing body through consolidation or, in the case of police and public works, for operating the public safety and public works departments under shared service agreements. Many departments had a number of options for restructuring ranging from the most conservative (no reduction in staffing) to aggressive (reductions in staffing and, in some cases, service delivery). While CGR provided a series of options, it was the commission that studied the options and developed its final recommendations.

Using the options report as a guideline, the commission members reviewed each department and conducted the majority of the work in subcommittees. Anton Lahnston, the commission chair, recognized that the commission would have to be organized and diligent in reviewing all the data and input from CGR, the municipal staff, the state and the community. To be most effective, he established a series of subcommittees within the consolidation commission to review each decision point and bring recommendations to a full vote of the commission.

Subcommittees were set up in the following areas:

- **Community Engagement Subcommittee** – This committee was charged with public outreach. Having researched the previous attempts to consolidate the Princeton community, commission members were aware that poor or delayed public communication contributed to misunderstandings of factual data. This committee arranged public meetings with major stakeholders in the community and held neighborhood meetings in each section of the borough and the township. By the time of the referendum in November of 2011, the community engagement subcommittee convened over 70 neighborhood and stakeholder meetings throughout the Princetons. Some of the most oft-repeated feedback from residents and stakeholders shared with the commission were:

    - Savings at equal levels for residents of both municipalities (i.e. fairness) – One town should not benefit to a significantly greater degree than the other.

    - Efficiencies in governmental operations – Responsiveness to community needs should increase, not decrease, as a result of consolidation.

    - No degradation of services (especially with police and public works) – Many residents liked the services they had and many also expressed a desire to improve services where possible without a commensurate increase in taxes.

    - Sense of community – This was seen as a negative for some residents, as they felt they would potentially 'lose' their sense of community in a consolidated town (see Boroughness). Others, however, felt that consolidation would bring a greater sense of community as the towns would no longer be working at cross-purposes.

- Perceived dilution of representation – This was mainly a concern among a small group of Princeton Borough residents who believed that they would be outvoted in a consolidated municipality. The group claimed that without wards, the representation on the consolidated governing body would be taken over by township residents. Their concern would later prove unwarranted, since the newly elected consolidated government actually had more former borough representatives than township representatives. The majority of voters refused to support a candidate solely based on which former municipality served as the candidate's residence.

- Transition Costs – Residents wanted to understand how much would it cost to make the transition to a single municipality. Even though there would be savings, how many years would it take to realize them with transition costs? The commission was also challenged in this area, as it was only possible to make estimates based on reports received from municipal staff.

- Simplicity – The residents made it clear that they appreciated the level of engagement to which the commission was committed. They wanted to make sure that the commission would clearly communicate its rationale for its recommendations and at the same time be transparent in doing so. The commission also maintained a website through CGR for posting all the commission's reports and meeting minutes.

- **Municipal Consolidation Subcommittee** – The municipal consolidation subcommittee focused on aspects related to the nuts and bolts of consolidation and the aspects of the Local Option Municipal Consolidation Act that could apply to this consolidation effort. In addition, one of the major projects for this subcommittee was to recommend the form of government for the new municipality. Eight options were possible, and the towns had to evaluate the merits of each one, including the use of wards.

- **Public Works Subcommittee** – Public works was another specific department to be evaluated as a potential shared service, if the commission failed to recommend full municipal consolidation. The subcommittee, therefore, took a deeper look at service delivery, optimum staff levels, and equipment sharing and storage options.

- **Police/Public Safety Subcommittee** – The biggest cost center for both municipalities and a potential candidate for a shared service in the absence of full consolidation were police services. This subcommittee studied how a combined police force could best serve the community. Looking at the baseline report and the options analysis from CGR, the committee looked at call statistics and crime responses in each community, savings that could result in combining dispatch and officer personnel, and labor contracts.

- **Finance Subcommittee** – The finance subcommittee looked at the financial savings of consolidation or a shared police and/or public works department. The committee worked directly with the New Jersey's Department of Community Affairs (DCA) to coordinate its financial analysis report with our consultant's analysis. The committee also determined the financial impact on the average resident in each town based on the total estimated savings and the impacts of equalizing the tax rates between the towns.

Each member of the commission and supporting staff from each town served on several of the subcommittees. To integrate the process and link communication between subcommittees, the chair of the commission attended every subcommittee meeting. It was an extremely effective way of focusing the efforts of the joint commission. Transparency was paramount, and all subcommittee meetings were open to the public. This served to build public trust and gather input that would be critical to a successful outcome.

While CGR was working on the options report, one of the most discussed areas of the consolidated town was the form of government. New Jersey has eight acceptable structures for a municipal governing unit [*see Government Structure Options Chart*].

The township operated under the 'township' form of government that does not have a directly elected mayor. It has five elected committeepersons who then elect a mayor and deputy mayor to serve each calendar year.

The borough had the aptly named 'borough' form of government. Although a borough is no longer a legal government structure for a newly formed municipality, it still could be a grandfathered government structure, since the borough government existed in one of the merging municipalities.

	Borough	Township	OMCL Mayor-Council	OMCL Council-Manager	OMCL Mayor-Council-Admin	Comm-ission	Municipal Manager
Directly Elected Mayor	Yes	No	Yes	Optional	Yes	No	No
Mayor Vote in Council	Ties, Veto	Votes	Voice, No Vote, Veto	Votes	Tie, Veto	Votes	Votes
Mayor Term of Office	4	1	4	4 or 2	4	4	4
Governing Body Size	6	3 or 5	5, 7 or 9	5, 7 or 9	6	5 if pop is > 12,000	3, 5, 7 or 9
Governing Body Presiding Officer	Mayor	Mayor	Council President	Mayor	Mayor	Mayor	Mayor
Governing Body Term of Office	3	3	4	4	3	4	4
Require Chief Administrator	No	No	Yes	Yes	Yes	No	Yes
Limit Staff Contact	No	No	Council	Mayor, Council	No	No	No
Use of Wards	No	No	Optional	Optional	No	No	No
Non-Partisan Elections	No	No	Optional	Optional	No	Yes	Yes
Staggered Terms	Yes	Yes	Optional	Optional	Yes	No	No
Initiative and Referendum	No	No	Yes	Yes	Yes	Yes	No

Government Structure Options Chart – CGR Options Report, Princeton 2011

Each form of government had its pluses and minuses from the perspectives of the two Princetons. But the Municipal Consolidation Subcommittee had several key criteria that were fundamental to its choice. First, the mayor had to be directly elected. Second, the form would have to allow all the elected officials to have access to professional staff. Some town government forms allowed only the mayor to have access to staff. Both the borough and the township elected officials were accustomed to having access to municipal staff; they believed that direct problem solving brought accountability to the governing structure.

The requirement of a directly elected mayor eliminated the township, commission and municipal manager forms of government. The requirement of staff access eliminated the Optional Municipal Charter Law (OMCL) forms of government, since those three forms restrict council's access to staff under the New Jersey State Administrative Code. [Municipal Subcommittee meeting minutes of February 10, 2011]

This left the committee with only two choices: 1) the borough form (grandfathered as a selection); and 2) a 'special charter' form of government.

The special charter is a create-your-own form of government. The commission looked at this because there was some level of interest in establishing wards in the newly consolidated town to preserve representation in certain geographies, and the borough form of government did not allow the use of wards.

Analysis, however, revealed that the wards would be ineffective in the consolidated municipality for two reasons: 1) it was impossible to define them prior to the consolidation referendum, thus leaving a gray area with voters; 2) it was unacceptable to draw the wards by using the old municipal boundaries and instead would have to use population bands with no consideration of the two towns' borders; and 3) wards, according to some, might contribute to divisiveness in a relatively small community that was trying to come together.

Complicating this, a special charter would be reliant upon approval by the NJ State Legislature. Even though the towns could create their own unique structure, it also risked the viability of the referendum because residents might be voting on a referendum for consolidation without a confirmation of the type of government they would operate under. As a result of these factors, the subcommittee unanimously recommended the borough form of government.

The Options Analysis report was completed by CGR in March of 2011. It was immediately posted online for public viewing, and a joint public meeting was scheduled. The commission then met at the same time the subcommittee meetings were taking place to evaluate and recommend specific options for each area of the potential merger. Each subcommittee would evaluate the combination of cost savings and services that were most desirable and make that option recommendation to the full commission. Meanwhile, the finance subcommittee would take each option and determine the total cost savings to a combined municipality.

Recommendations and Report to Joint Governing Bodies

At the end of the options phase, the finance subcommittee estimated a total savings of approximately $3.1 million at full implementation or a reduction of five percent of total municipal spending. This was a significant savings. It would allow for additional services to be provided in the community, as well as allow for greater budget flexibility to slow the rate of tax increases in the newly combined Princeton community.

The commission chose a three-year implementation process, because of the structure of the police force. The demographics of the police force allowed for staffing reductions through attrition and made the three-year period optimal. The commission approved and presented the governing bodies with a solid draft plan.

Throughout this thoughtful and thorough decision-making process, however, the opposition was coalescing as it did in 1996. Preserve Our Historic Borough was back, and it was out to disable any attempt to consolidate. To complicate matters further, several issues facing the towns had the potential of sabotaging a successful outcome.

Beavers and Boroughness, Oh My!

"As I peruse the local press, I am struck by the ominous headlines of recent weeks. Bad beavers, rabid raccoons, boorish bears, and the ubiquitous deer (up to their usual devastation of SUVs and pricey shrubbery). Rumors and alarms abound, citing the appearance of coyotes, panthers, and fisher cats. Can wolves and alligators be far behind?...It could well be that someone overcome with an irrational feeling of 'Boroughness' is trying to conjure up the specter of a terroristic township takeover, spearheaded by a cadre of militant mammals."

– **Bill Moran**, "Letter to the Editor," Town Topics, August 20, 2011

As an elected official, I found that working in local government had its moments. Certainly, working on a large scale, transformative project like consolidation was at times engaging and interesting – and bizarre. In addition to whatever wacky element consolidation brought to our plates, we also had day-to-day issues and events to address.

Boroughness

Princeton Borough was a small community of 1.8 square miles and about 12,000 residents., It was completely surrounded by Princeton Township, comprising 16.5 square miles and some 16,000 residents. Many residents would be unable to identify where the borough ended and the township began. Yet, the prospect of consolidation in each attempt was enough to draw some members of the borough into feeling a distinct sense of so-called boroughness that brought out fear of consolidation and somehow a distinctly separate feeling with the surrounding township.

Fear of change is the biggest intangible that can dismantle any consolidation effort. Some aspects of the fear can be addressed, and others are more challenging. One borough resident declared that there might be a true cultural difference between the borough and the township, because the township officials sit higher on a dais than the borough officials:

"Consider and compare the main auditorium in the borough with that of the township. In the borough, the dais is elevated so that the seated Mayor and Council will be at about the same eye level as a member of the audience standing at the microphone. The effect is that the audience member is speaking with his elected peers as equals. By contrast, the new Township auditorium has the dais raised much higher, so that the elected representatives look down on the person standing at the microphone. Do we borough residents really want to replace communicating as equals with our elected officials with pleading to the commissars at the presidium? Yes, there may be a cultural difference..." – **Borough resident Ron Nielsen** in a memo to Princeton Future (a community grassroots group advocating for smart growth and culturally sensitive planning).

This "cultural difference" was embedded in a nebulous term called boroughness. What is boroughness? Honestly, I am unsure but believe it is an intangible term equating an emotional attachment to a borough resident's sense of place. Is it real? I guess it depends on one's perspective. Did it potentially jeopardize a successful consolidation attempt? Yes. In fact, the anti-consolidation group from 1996, 1991, and even 1979 was called "Preserve Our Historic Borough (POHB)." They were beginning to ramp up their opposition to consolidation effort even before the commission finished its work and presented its recommendations. Several opponents focused on boroughness and the distinct "character" of the borough or "cultural differences" between the two towns. Some of the fears relating to boroughness were:

- Getting "outvoted" by Princeton Township – This pre-supposes that there is one single issue that would cause all voters in the former township to vote the opposite way from the borough. Although hardly a likely event, this concern was taken seriously and addressed by the consolidation commission and the Unite Princeton campaign. The new, single governing body post-election, however, would nullify the premise for this concern.

- Walking versus driving culture – POHB noted that borough residents lived closer to the central business district and were more of a walking culture, while the township residents were a driving culture. This insinuated a cultural difference between the two municipalities.

- Central business district – The central business district was the common center for both the borough and the township, yet some in the borough believed that a combined government with township residents would fail to value and represent the central business district.

The JSSCC, seriously considering the boroughness issue, held several meetings with a design psychologist to better understand the emotional attachment to the sense of place expressed by some borough residents. The psychologist showed them that those attachments may exist independently of a separate government, and more than likely, the emotional attachment arose out of a sense of community and neighborhood. Still, *The Star-Ledger* newspaper mocked the whole boroughness concept by sending a reporter to the borough on a nice day and asking residents and visitors if they were "out enjoying the boroughness."

Once consolidation was recommended, however, the JSSCC thoroughly addressed rather than dismissed the concept of boroughness. The commissioners built rebuttals of the borough concerns into their presentations.

Beavergate

One result of the decades of consolidation attempts was a myriad of shared services between Princeton Township and Princeton Borough. From the early 1900s until the referendum on consolidation in 2011, Princeton was a state a leader in shared services. As mentioned previously, shared services refer to departments that serve both towns, and the costs are shared between the two municipalities. A board or commission, especially the one in charge of the larger shared service departments, reports to each governing body. In many cases the smaller departments are simply administered by one of the two respective towns. Elected officials sometimes favor shared services over a merger, because the town's home rule stays intact. In practice, shared services can sometimes be a source of headaches and finger-pointing (a.k.a., grandstanding) for elected officials in either town.

Animal Control, usually a small department, is a common shared service between towns, recognizing that efficiencies can be gained from sharing one or several animal control officers. Princeton Borough and Princeton Township shared animal control, which was administered in Princeton Borough. It was normally a very quiet department that responded to the animal infractions across the Princeton community, such as bats in the attic, rabid raccoons, deer stuck in fencing, and other wildlife engaged in adventures within the quasi-urban community.

In 2011, the year the JSSCC was gearing up for the referendum on consolidation, shared service frustration reared its head. The event occurred close to my home adjacent to the Pettoranello Gardens in Mountain Lakes Park on a small cul-de-sac. My neighbors and I would use the park daily, and many of us discovered a new wildlife attraction: beavers. Scores of neighbors would observe the beavers swimming around the island in a small lake within Pettoranello Gardens.

One early evening in May 2011, my neighbor was walking in the park and heard shots fired. The animal control officer killed two beavers because of a departmental concern that the beavers were contributing to the area's flooding problem. Many residents were outraged, and that outrage spread to national animal protection groups. As mayor, I received letters from animal activists all over the country.

I asked for a full investigation of why this happened and wanted to reassure residents that it was safe to walk in the park at dusk. The event devolved into what residents called "Beavergate." The problem with getting to the bottom of what happened was that the land and location of the incident was Princeton Township. Princeton Borough and the Princeton Regional Health Commission administered animal control. I got mired in evasive bureaucratic responses, while simultaneously being bombarded by communication from outraged residents and national animal protection groups.

Eventually, the animal control officer was accused of a minor offense of shooting two beavers in Pettoranello Gardens without a state permit. The beavers were classified as a nuisance by animal control because they were contributing to the flooding of the pond. The animal control officer failed to obtain state authorization to shoot the beavers and had no a permit to trap and euthanize the beavers (one cannot trap and relocate beavers – I learned this as I became a beaver expert).

Trying to resolve an issue such as Beavergate was particularly frustrating, because the multiple jurisdictional authorities added to the slowness in responding to residents' concerns. A local online media site, _Planet Princeton_, summed up the whole debacle:

"In response to the beaver shootings, Princeton adopted new wildlife guidelines detailed in a three-inch thick manual that lists how each animal is supposed to be handled, from beavers to snakes to feral cats." [_Planet Princeton_ (planetprinceton.com) October 13, 2011]

That's right: the towns followed up the investigation with a new *three-inch thick* manual.

The Train Goes Off The Rails

"I'm not going to throw my colleagues in the borough under the train."

– **Township Committeewoman Sue Nemeth,** "Princeton University, Officials Remain in Stalemate Over $300 million Arts and Transit Project," The Times of Trenton, February 7, 2011

While concerned about the intangible boroughness issue as a threat to bringing the communities together, I was equally worried about how other big and very tangible issues affecting both towns could pull the communities apart.

Princeton University's Arts & Transit proposal had been a hot topic for community discussion throughout 2010, and 2011 was to be the year of decisions. Princeton University had unveiled its campus plan in 2006. It included an unpopular idea of moving the existing "Dinky" (small shuttle train connecting the town of Princeton to the Northeast Corridor Transit hub at Princeton Junction) train station 460 feet south. This move would bring the Dinky station further from the center of town and out of the borough and into the township. In the four years since the unveiling of the campus plan, the governing body members met informally with the university for briefings on the university's proposed project.

In the beginning of 2011, municipal approvals for the project were going nowhere. Most, if not all, of the opposition centered on the existing station terminus moving further from the Central Business District. Planning experts held that an inviolable urban planning rule is that transit always should be as close as possible to the center of retail and business activities. Both municipalities had been reviewing their options to prevent a movement of the station and secure long-term viability for mass transit to serve the

community. This review was holding up the zoning that the university needed to move forward.
The university was becoming impatient. Its president, donors and senior administrators had waited four years for the town to take action. However, they failed to acknowledge in the plans the fact that moving the Dinky station was extremely unpopular.

On January 31, 2011, the governing bodies held a joint meeting to hear from the university about its Arts & Transit project and allow input from the community. Princeton University President Shirley Tilghman in her presentation struck a strident tone and began with comments that only served to cast a pall over the town/gown relationship:

"It is a rare occasion when the president of the university appears before the governing bodies of the borough and the township. It is rare when borough council and township committee meet together, and do so with the planning board. And it is rare when an issue needs to be addressed that is as important as this one to the university, to the community, and to the relationship between the two," she said.

It should be a common rather than rare occasion for the university president to appear in front of the governing bodies. The fact that this meeting was so unusual highlighted the glaring disconnect between the president's view and the view of the elected officials.

The Arts & Transit project was made possible because of a very significant gift from Progressive Insurance executive Peter Lewis, Princeton class of 1955 (d. 2013). President Tilghman, responding to the donor's desire to see the project go forward in a timely fashion, felt frustrated by the towns' inaction. The project needed zoning changes from the governing bodies. Complicating approvals was the fact that the project spanned both the township and the borough. Both governing bodies had to agree to the changes. But the elected officials, feeling pressure from residents unhappy with the university's plans, were frustrated by the university's lack of flexibility regarding the controversial move of the Dinky station.

President Tilghman's exasperation with the process led to the following statement:

"For Peter Lewis, whose historic gift was meant to create those opportunities, I owe him the realization of his vision. If, after you have heard our description of this plan for an arts and transit neighborhood, and the many benefits that we believe it brings to this community, you conclude that you will not be willing to move forward to put zoning in place to allow us to proceed, I will instruct my colleagues tomorrow to begin planning for another site for the Lewis Center. If you conclude you cannot decide to move forward, I will be forced to give them the same instruction. This is a 'go-no-go' moment for the University this evening."

We probably could have closed the meeting after that statement. I noticed the body language of the governing bodies change and they were not going to simply provide a blanket approval without addressing the issue of the Dinky station. The meeting ended with no action. The next day, *The Princeton Packet* ran the headline "University To Abandon Site For Arts District." [February 1, 2011]

Many on the governing bodies were surprised to see the university attempt to pull out of the Arts & Transit project and look for an alternative location for it. Elected officials were aware that the university had expended a considerable amount of time and money developing its plans for that site. Some felt like we owed it to everyone involved to sit down and try to negotiate some type of understanding regarding the Dinky Station and secure the long-term viability of the train - and by doing so generate enough support to move the project forward.

I reached out to the university with Princeton Borough Mayor Mildred Trotman, and we created a small committee to negotiate with the university. There would be two representatives from each municipality and several from Princeton University in an attempt to address the long-term concerns of the Dinky shuttle train. We would meet over a finite term and try to hammer out a Memorandum of Understanding (MOU).

Township representatives were Bernie Miller and myself; borough representatives were Kevin Wilkes and Roger Martindell. Several members of the borough council were rigid in their opposition to the station moving; and any agreement that we brought back to our respective governing bodies had a high probability of being shot down.

I believe that no one on either governing body wanted to see the station moved further south away from town. Some were more strident than others. Also, there was considerable disagreement among the members on the governing bodies about how to go about resolving the issue. The university had a 1984 agreement with New Jersey Transit; and that agreement contained a clause about a one-time right to relocate the Dinky terminus.

Princeton Township and Princeton Borough were not parties to that 1984 agreement, however. Some maintained that the university had already exercised a one-time right to move the station by moving it to the southern end of the platform. Others argued that the towns could sue the university to prevent a move, because New Jersey Transit would be failing to act in the 'public interest' by allowing the 460-foot move. Either way, both contentions could be forced only via a lawsuit that would be costly for the municipalities and the outcome would be quite uncertain.

Still others discussed having one municipality or both declare eminent domain to seize the existing station and the land providing the existing right of way. This action would have been unprecedented not to mention extremely costly for the municipalities. This too would be unable to prevent New Jersey Transit and Princeton University from moving the terminus further south, as one who owns the land does not own the tracks.

Some suggested that we could refuse to zone the property for the higher density needed by the university to redevelop the site for the arts complex. This action would have the effect of thwarting the project, but still would do nothing to stop a further southern movement of the station at some later date.

The community consensus in both municipalities was to keep the station in its current location – and both governing bodies in the township and the borough shared that objective. However, that neither solved the long-term viability of the Dinky service nor was it something that the municipalities could control or demand. The only solution had to involve Princeton University – the owner of the station and the land under the existing tracks at its current terminus.

After a long, arduous negotiation and several fits and starts in the fall of 2011, we were able to bring a Memorandum of Understanding (MOU) back to the respective governing bodies for consideration.

For the first time ever, the MOU brought together Princeton Borough and Township and Princeton University in a binding agreement. The university was bound never to initiate a move of the station further south (or further from the center of town) after implementing the 460-foot relocation without local government approval.

In addition, the MOU provided for dedicated shuttles to meet peak commuter trains at the new station and bring them to the center of town and beyond. Certainly this was a compromise – short of the ideal outcome of no movement of the station, but better than nothing. The most important thing was making the town a party to any further movement of the station, thus giving the municipalities control over the station's location and insuring that the station never would be moved again without local government approval. We could enhance the Dinky and secure its long-term viability and plan alternative transportation solutions for the corridor.

Several members of borough council opposed the MOU. The opposition was problematic for the upcoming consolidation referendum, because the issue of moving the Dinky was conflated with the issue of boroughness.

Borough Councilwoman Jenny Crumiller wrote an op/ed in Planet Princeton and used the word "boroughness." She wrote in opposition to the Memorandum of Understanding:

"And one final point on the value of the Dinky may be particularly relevant. There has been much talk in the consolidation debate about boroughness - that intangible quality valued by borough residents that was given a name in community meetings. We're already losing the Palmer Square post office. We shouldn't also lose another one of the most important contributors to boroughness. Taking a ride on the Dinky is boroughness." [*Planet Princeton* (planetprinceton.com), "Op-Ed: Transit Agreement With Princeton University A Bad Deal For Residents," October 05, 2011]

I admired the principled objection. The only problem was that it could morph into a township versus borough issue, and in doing so, undermine the consolidation vote. Residents in both communities valued and continue to value the Dinky. Township residents loved the Dinky. Many township residents were behind the Save-The-Dinky advocacy organization. The issue was that there were some members of borough council who never would accept the station moving at any cost. This did not make it a borough or township issue – it was a principled political objection that would have occurred whether or not the towns were consolidated.

I was focused on preventing the train from derailing the prospects of consolidation. The Unite Princeton campaign team put together a flyer that tackled the issue of the Dinky being just a borough issue. The MOU was ultimately passed by the borough, and township shortly before the consolidation referendum – thus avoiding a potential obstacle.

Want to save the Dinky and downtown?

Then vote *FOR* consolidation.

- **A strong voice for in-town residents**: In a united Princeton, a majority of the population will consist of current Borough residents and their close neighbors from the Township who reside within walking distance of the downtown such as on Birch Ave, Jefferson Rd, etc.

- **More options to strengthen and preserve the downtown:** Consolidation will lead to added budget flexibility, more revenue options, and unified planning. This is key to preserving the historic Princeton Borough and its businesses.

- **Protecting neighborhood character:** Consolidation will allow creation of Advisory Planning Districts to give each neighborhood an official voice in front of our zoning and planning boards.

- **Accountability:** The Township and Borough are inextricably linked, and decisions made by the governing body of one municipality can impact the residents of the other. With consolidation, all the politicians will be accountable to the whole community.

Consolidation gives us a stronger voice in dealing with Princeton University and other 3rd parties – it protects us from a divide-and-conquer strategy.

Paid for by Unite Princeton. PO Box 1366, Princeton, NJ 08542. Visit us at **www.uniteprinceton.org** or find us on Facebook.

Unite Princeton Dinky Ad from the 2011 Campaign

Unite Princeton!

"Don't be Myth-Led!"

– 2011 Unite Princeton flyer and advertisement

The multiple consolidation attempts from 1953 to 1996 made one thing very clear: in order to have a chance at a successful consolidation referendum, the towns must have an organized campaign that goes beyond coordination of letters-to-the editor and campaign advertisements in the local newspapers.

Shortly after the Joint Shared Services and Consolidation Commission (JSSCC) voted to recommend consolidation, there was an effort to form a campaign group to combat what would certainly be an anti-consolidation group. In 1979, 1991, and 1996, formal anti-consolidation groups were formed. We anticipated that many of the residents involved in those efforts back then would be back this time around.

Early meetings focused on getting volunteers and preparing a timeline for key points along the campaign. First, the core consolidation group had to come up with a name. 'One Princeton' was not an option, as that was the name of the group in 1996, and the name United Princeton sounded like a professional soccer team. Ultimately, they decided to call it Unite Princeton. Pro-consolidation volunteers led by the Liz Lempert, Peter Wolanin, Dan Preston, Jenny Crumiller and others would spend the next months organizing a voter mobilization effort. Liz was deputy mayor in the township and a veteran of voter outreach in Mercer County with the Obama campaign, and Peter was involved in the local municipal Democratic Committee and a whiz in technology and voter data.

The key difference between Unite Princeton and the other attempts at consolidation in Princeton was that the principals within Unite Princeton conducted not only a robust advertising campaign, but also a smart political campaign. They created voter lists, conducted phone banking, made campaign door hangers, buttons and stickers, and held sign-up tables at high traffic areas of town to recruit volunteers. Specifically, they organized the following:

- Volunteer sign-ups and issue awareness events – Known as 'tabling', Unite Princeton put up tables at well-traveled areas of town, like Hinds Plaza near the public library and the Princeton Shopping Center. The goal was to: raise awareness of the consolidation commission's recommendation and the upcoming referendum; hand out flyers promoting consolidation of the two towns; and sign-up like-minded volunteers to help with phone-banking, literature drops, and other campaign activities.

- Voter lists and phone banking – Perhaps one of the most important parts of a referendum campaign is micro-targeting - learning who your voters are and which ones are the most likely to show up and vote. Unite Princeton used the county voter database to determine likely voters. Using headquarters space donated by local architect Bob Hillier, volunteers contacted those voters and asked them to vote to support consolidation. The phone-bankers also identified those individuals who supported consolidation for potential future contact and mailings and disregarded those who were against consolidation. The calculus was that by ignoring anti-consolidation residents, they would be less motivated to vote.

- Campaign door hangers, signs, and buttons – Building visual awareness is also an important component of any campaign. Aside from talking up consolidation at the tabling events in town, signs and bumper stickers with the Unite Princeton logo created a sense of broad community support. In addition, the door hangers were used to provide key bullet points on why to support consolidation and to counteract flyer drops from the anti-consolidation group.

- Advertisements and letters-to-the-editor – Newspaper advertisements designed by Unite Princeton focused on two key areas: combatting myths and rumors with fact-based data from the consolidation commission and providing testimonials in support of consolidation from local officials and prominent Princetonians. In addition, the letters-to-the-editor were coordinated to ensure a steady stream of community support in the local papers.

Previous consolidation efforts taught the value of a rapid response to rumors or accusations. The Unite Princeton was extremely proactive to ensure that either through advertisements, mailings and/or letters-to-the-editor, no negative comment, rumor or myth on consolidation went unanswered.

Perhaps the most impactful response to the anti-consolidation rumor-mill was an ad entitled "Don't Be Myth-Led." It was a direct response to anti-consolidation flyers that were circulating. It emphasized some of the key reasons why consolidation made sense, because it would save money and would be more effective and efficient at delivering services. This also tied in to a presentation made by the JSSCC chair Anton Lahnston to the joint governing bodies entitled 'Myths vs. Reality' in September of 2011.

Don't be Myth-Led!

Consolidation is a win for the Borough and our entire community.

FACT: Every Borough and Township resident will save on his or her municipal tax bill.

FACT: Borough and Township residents will continue to receive the same or better services as they have today.

FACT: All residents will gain a voice in zoning decisions through a single, accountable government.

FACT: In-town voters will make up the majority in a consolidated municipality, strengthening representation for the downtown.

FACT: Advisory planning districts will unite and provide standing to neighborhoods in a consolidated municipality.

FACT: The Borough has depleted its capital surplus for the last several years in order to keep taxes flat. Without consolidation, taxes are sure to increase.

Consolidation delivers approximately $4.8M per year in benefits to our combined community. For more facts see www.cgr.org/princeton.

Vote YES on November 8th

Join us! Visit **uniteprinceton.org** or email Peter Wolanin at info@uniteprinceton.org.

Paid for by Unite Princeton · John Borden, Treasurer · PO Box 1366 Princeton, NJ 08542

Police and Donuts

"Doughnuts are good for eating, but not for living in."

– **anonymous Princeton resident,** Planet Princeton (planetprinceton.com), November 8, 2011

As the fall of 2011 approached, Unite Princeton was in full swing and comfortable with its strategy of promoting a 'yes' vote on the referendum and combatting the POHB opposition campaign. A few hurdles knocked us out of the comfort zone, but never into despair - no matter how challenged.

Leading up to the recommendation to consolidate from the JSSCC, the police departments of both towns had been extremely cooperative. In general, the two departments were not keen on consolidation, shared services or other efforts of cooperation between them, but they had been willing and active participants in the consolidation commission's work.

As the fall campaign began to intensify, I awoke one morning to find a letter from the township's police union urging residents in the township to vote against consolidation. Arriving in every township voter's mailbox, the letter began: "As responsible members of the community we also feel it is our duty to inform you about potential public safety concerns we have in regards to consolidation" and went on to list concerns centered around the proposed reduction in police personnel in a combined municipality.

The letter stated that according to national standards a consolidated Princeton should have a police department of a minimum of 66 officers, yet even in the two separate towns at the time of the referendum vote they had only 60 officers between them. A consolidated town with the ability to eliminate or reduce middle management staffing should have more officers? It made no sense; the statistics they quoted failed to consider the vastly low crime rate in the Princetons.

Next, the letter sought to raise the angst level among the township residents, by saying that the downtown service calls would deprive the township of officers to patrol neighborhoods and would produce an overall slower response time. In stark contrast, the commission's research anticipated none of this.

Furthermore, none of this has transpired post-consolidation. The letter referred to a reduction in dispatch service, but failed to mention that a combined dispatch is more efficient and could better serve the whole Princeton community.

It was a shocking, blindside that could have undermined our entire consolidation initiative. I decided to be proactive and contact the newspapers to combat the letter and dispel the fears.

I responded in an interview with *Planet Princeton*: "I can understand that our force is concerned about staff reductions, that is why it was important that we performed this review with independent consultants while at the same time gathering input from the two municipal police chiefs. The consolidation commission has called for a smaller, yet effective and efficient force under a consolidated municipality. It is understandable staffing reductions can generate fear in the department and those fears can be projected in the forms of union letters, and studies." [*Planet Princeton* (planetprinceton.com), "Princeton Township Police Union Lobbies Against Consolidation," October 27, 2011]

I also pointed out that the figures and data from the police letter came from a study that was performed for the police union pro bono by the New Jersey Police Officers Association. I compared the veracity of that data with the commission's consultant whom our own township police department had hired a few years ago to update the police policy manual. If the department trusted the consultant for a previous task, the police should have trusted the same consultant and his recommendations to the consolidation study commission. The commission's recommendation to reduce the combined police department staffing from 60 officers to 51 officers over three years could most likely be achieved through normal attrition.

The key challenges faced by the municipal government was trying to manage costs and keep taxes low. "Our fixed costs continue to rise at rates higher than inflation, driven by state pension costs and health care costs, all while we operate under the constraints of a two-percent municipal cap. A consolidated police department will deliver services more effectively and at a lower cost to our community. And in times of emergency, a consolidated department will unify our resources, create a single dispatch center to eliminate confusion and create a single line of command in emergency response." [**Chad Goerner**, "Princeton Township Police Union Lobbies Against Consolidation," *Planet Princeton* (planetprinceton.com), October 27, 2011]

When it comes to police and public works services, there are additional service benefits and efficiencies that can be achieved above and beyond just cost savings. As we saw with our hurricane response and emergency response, a combined dispatch increases the safety and security for our residents. I continued to press the issue right up to the election: "It's about balancing public safety with having a single line of command and saving $2.1 million a year. I think the commission has made a very strong case resulting in not only significant savings, but also improved services and a more accountable governing structure."

Undeterred by this setback, I volunteered to go door to door in the borough each weekend up to the election. I spoke with voters, left literature, and continued to press on with the campaign. Unite Princeton's campaign had a busy team of volunteers calling voters and walking the streets to promote a Yes vote on November 8th. At the same time, the anti-consolidation group was also going door to door. The difference was that they were using some pretty scary advertising again:

POHB Ad and Flyer used in the 2011 referendum campaign

Election day was upon us. After the polls closed on election day, Princeton Democrats traditionally met at Conte's pizzeria to see the election returns. Having spent thousands of hours to move the towns toward consolidation, I was anxious that it could be all for naught.

Arriving at Conte's, I witnessed a packed house of excited residents as the returns started to come in. Once the first few precincts reported, it was clear that it was going to pass this time and by a wide margin. The township voted 85 percent to consolidate, 3,542 to 604. The borough had a significant majority in favor as well with about 61 percent voting to consolidate 1,238 to 828.

Anton Lahnston, the chair of the JSSCC, was ecstatic. "I spent so many sleepless nights wondering what else we could have done to make it happen, but we did it," Mr. Lahnston said, as he stood on a chair and addressed the crowd. "Thanks to all who kept the faith." [**Anton Lahnston**, "Princeton Trailblazers Vote to Unite," *Planet Princeton* (planetprinceton.com), November 8, 2011]

We overcame six decades of consolidation defeats and struggles and many said it would never happen. Interviewed by *The Times of Trenton*, I said: "Princeton decided it wanted to be a leader tonight. Reason over fear won out when it came to the polls." [**Chad Goerner**, "Princeton Borough, Township Approve Question To Merge Towns," *The Times of Trenton*, November 8, 2011]

Close to Conte's where the celebration was going on, Preserve Our Historic Borough was having its own election-night watch. After I left Conte's, I went with Deputy Mayor Liz Lempert to visit Kate and Benjamin "Roz" Warren, two of the leaders of that group, at their home to let them both know that they put up a good fight. Even though we disagreed as to the solution for the future of the towns, I hoped we could begin the process of healing and putting this contentious issue behind us. They were both able to do that. While some issues have lingered in the newly consolidated Princeton, their dedication to the town and its values are to be applauded.

PART TWO

A Template for Successful Shared Services and Consolidation Efforts

The Transition and a Look Back

"Borough resident Claire Jacobus expressed dismay at the level of bad feeling this latest effort to consolidate has generated, and Mr. Goerner may have had that same concern in mind when, earlier in the meeting, he described a recent talk he had with a Littlebrook Elementary School fifth grade class. Asked to define 'consolidation,' one student suggested that it had to do with 'putting an arm around a friend and saying it'll be okay.'"

– **A Littlebrook Elementary School fifth-grader,** "Township and Borough Engage One Last Time In Discussions For and Against Consolidation," Town Topics, November 2, 2011

With the successful referendum now behind us, January 2012 began the "transition year" – the year in which Princeton Borough and Princeton Township still would operate as separate towns but use their time to organize staffing, ordinances and budgets to prepare for operating as a single municipality in January of 2013.

The towns created a new transition task force, an advisory commission that would recommend organizational structures, benefit harmonization and implement the recommendations of the Joint Shared Services and Consolidation Commission (JSSCC). The task force had four residents and two elected officials from each municipality. Candidates were invited to join the task force by an open call for applications/resumes.

Mark Freda, a former Princeton Borough councilman and dedicated town volunteer, chaired it. Mimicking the consolidation commission, additional subcommittees were created and additional volunteers were brought in from the community to help with the various implementation tasks in the areas of personnel, public safety (police), communications and community outreach, finance, public works, engineering and recreation.

The work that the members of the transition task force and its subcommittees performed was significant. Administratively, there were boards and commissions to merge, ordinances to review and prioritize for harmonization, organizational structures to formalize, aligning staff benefits in and much more. Many tasks were particularly challenging, requiring a deft balance as the decisions involved municipal staff. The staff had already been on edge and concerned, because the combination of the towns involved staffing reductions to generate efficiencies and cost savings, and it was hard to deal with benefit and organizational concerns as well.

The members of the task force were not fully up to speed on the recommendations and reports put forth by the Joint Shared Services and Consolidation Commission. It led to some mission creep and as a result, the task force's consultant, again the Center for Governmental Research (CGR), was called upon to design and implement a task map to help the task force prioritize its duties. This helped to refocus the task force and, ultimately, after some bumps it began to make a significant contribution to the implementation of consolidation.

Looking back at the transition process, the Graduate Student Consulting Group, chaired by Logan Clark at the Woodrow Wilson School at Princeton University, analyzed the transition management in Princeton. These graduate student consultants recommended retaining the consolidation commission members, administrative staff and elected officials to implement the consolidation transition, because the commission members would have the institutional memory to ease the transition. In hindsight, that would have been preferable, but it may have been a challenge to accomplish. Consolidation commission members contributed a significant amount of time and effort since 2010, and there was a strong chance that some members would have refused to continue with a different mission of transition. Yet, in future consolidation efforts, retaining the consolidation commission for implementation may make sense.

Because of the task force's concerted efforts on staffing, benefits and other transition issues, savings from consolidation were even greater than the consolidation commission anticipated. The transition finance subcommittee's projections determined personnel savings levels for year one (2013) that were at least 40 percent greater than the joint commission's original estimates - $2.26 million vs. $1.61 million. In addition, at the three-year full implementation of consolidation (end of 2015), savings projections provided the new governing body with the opportunity to exceed the original savings estimates projected by the consolidation commission. Just like the consolidation commission recommendations, the savings projections provided by the transition task force were contingent on follow through from the new governing body. Three years later, these money saving benefits were even more impressive than the task force had anticipated.

A Model

"Today is the day when we start to build a unified future as Princetonians. When we come together and support one another we can do great things. We can turn a page and start a new chapter. What will be the story of that new chapter? Will it be a cautionary tale, or will we be a model for consolidation? There can only be one answer to that question. We will succeed."

– **Princeton Mayor Liz Lempert, the first mayor of consolidated Princeton,** "Reorganization Address,"– January 2013

From 1952 to 2011, Princeton Borough and Princeton Township were engaged in a decades-long affair flirting with consolidation and shared services. Each of the failed attempts provided wisdom and experience that we would apply to the next attempt ultimately resulting in the 2011 success.

- In 1953, the commission and the public failed to take an active role in engaging in the referendum until just before the vote. That was partly due to the commission being formed in the beginning of that year and working quickly - their report came out in May with a referendum that fall. That short timeline never allowed for vetting all public concerns. Coupled with the rumors of the disbanding of the fire department and the uncertainty regarding the financial impacts, each town rejected consolidation.

- In 1965, the Joint Report on Municipal Operations was favorable to consolidation. The towns, however, had widely different tax rates that would have resulted in the residents of one town gaining a significant advantage over the residents of the other town, when they would merge. This issue of tax rate equalization is a real one that exists to this day without a clear remedy. Only additional legislative action can address this issue effectively. Also, because of the tax-rate issue, the committee recommended a joint regional planning board and a joint health commission in lieu of immediate consolidation. However, it would not be until the turn of the decade that these joint solutions would be implemented.

One consolidation action did occur in the mid 1960s - the regionalization of the Princeton school system. This effort was dramatic and intense. The first vote to combine the school system failed. With immediate regret and outrage, the community put forth a new slate of school board candidates and another referendum on school district consolidation that finally was approved by the voters the following year. This underscored the need for a sustained, proactive issue campaign organization.

- In 1979, the next time consolidation made it to a vote, the referendum lost by only 33 votes in Princeton Borough. This effort was likely closer than in 1953, because the commission had completed a more thorough analysis of the financial impacts of consolidation and a more detailed analysis of the organizational structure of a combined town, service delivery and benefits of consolidation. In addition, the effort did have a more robust citizens' committee to campaign for consolidation. The rumor mill, however, was potent, and the consolidation effort ended with a borough rejection.

- In 1996, an ambitious commission put together a comprehensive recommendation to consolidate. It outlined a series of significant benefits to a combined community that built upon the report from the 1979 commission. However, the effort was also besieged by an aggressive anti-consolidation campaign that was characterized by myths, also known today as "fake news." It was difficult for the pro-consolidation effort to overcome emotionally charged misstatements put forth by the opposition. In addition, an independent consultant would be critical for providing the necessary data to the commission and the community in order to strengthen the credibility of the commission's recommendations.

This time around, if we were going to be successful we had to learn from our past. We had to assess how a new study effort could address any past obstacles or concerns so that we could garner wide acceptance among community leaders and stakeholders.

- ***An independent consultant*** to analyze financial data and provide unbiased data to the community was paramount. Princeton was blessed with wonderful minds and a large talent pool to analyze the proposed merger of the borough and the township. An independent consultant, however, would take the emotion out of the equation and also would help the commission avoid having its financial analysis and data tainted as "biased" by those opposing consolidation.

- ***The integration of elected officials and citizen representatives on the consolidation commission*** would help garner broad support. Elected officials are often the biggest obstacles to consolidation. Their support, however, is critical. They are the voice of the local government, and they can make any attempt to consolidate or share services incredibly difficult. Yet, they bring the institutional experience and understanding of the inner workings of government that can be valuable to a commission. Further, if elected officials are included on the commission, they may be less apt to undercut the recommendations or question the work of the commission.

- ***A comprehensive and coordinated issue campaign*** is essential. In past referendums, rumors and myths could overwhelm a well-organized campaign of newspaper advertisements and letters-to-the-editor. In order to increase the chances of success, we would need a proactive, rapid response campaign to dispel myths and rumors about consolidation directly and promote the positive benefits that it held for the community.

The Local Option Municipal Consolidation Act (2007) emerging from the past failed efforts in the Princetons provided some assistance to New Jersey municipalities considering consolidation. At the time, grants were available to help offset the cost of an independent consultant. New Jersey currently has limited funds available for pursuing consolidation or shared service studies. Other states, such as New York, have a pool of funds available to aid consolidation and regionalized service studies. If a state does not have the funds to begin a consolidation or shared services study, the towns may agree to fund the study jointly or a citizens group can fundraise to help get things off the ground.

The following is a framework to begin a dialogue on shared services or consolidation. It is based on a white paper that I wrote with the Princeton Joint Shared Services and Consolidation Commission (JSSCC) chair, Anton Lahnston and Joseph Stefko at the Center for Governmental Research (CGR).

Getting Started

- *Understand your community's history and identify obstacles*

Consolidation has proven its benefits to the Princeton community through cost savings, increased responsiveness and more efficient service delivery. Before getting started, however, it was important to identify and address at the beginning the obstacles and objections that arose from previous efforts. What has been your town's experience in working with neighboring towns? Do you share any services currently or have some level of collaboration?

If relations have been rocky between two towns, but there is some belief that working together on consolidation and/or shared services may make sense, begin with an informal dialogue with elected officials from both municipalities. Understand what has been holding them back and understand how the communities have worked together in the past. Then, you either can build on those strengths or determine the weaknesses. In Princeton, we began with a series of op/ed articles in the local paper to outline the concept and answer basic questions for residents. It helped establish a foundation and forge relations with both municipalities.

- *Establish a commission/committee with clearly defined operating procedures*

A committee will oversee the planning process, determine the scope of a consolidation and/or shared service study, and guide it to conclusion and recommendation for voter and/or governing body action. An effective committee is dependent on members with a diverse set of skills and the ability to thrive in a team environment.

In a consolidation or shared services effort, the committees should have equal representation from each town. In addition, having a combination of elected officials (one or two from each town) and resident members is crucial. CGR, the consultant to the Princetons, stated that elected officials "establish process legitimacy, have knowledge of governance, and ensure the governments' involvement;" and citizen representatives "lend 'outside' objectivity and a public voice." [**The Center For Governmental Research**, "Developing A Framework For Successful Government Efficiency", 2013]

A commission should resist the temptation to have too many members. More than 12 can be a recipe for inaction and subject the commission to losing focus. Instead, a smaller commission of six to 12 members can establish a series of subcommittees. The Princeton Joint Shared Services and Consolidation Commission (JSSCC) led by chair Anton Lahnston created a series of subcommittees to drive workflow up to the main commission. In the subcommittees, commissions can have subject matter experts, municipal staff and even other citizen representatives participate.

Once the commission has been established, a set of by-laws should be written to establish a quorum, define the rules of order, etc. Establishing a quorum is particularly important, because the municipalities must maintain equal representation. The use of 'alternate' members to fill in if a member cannot attend a meeting increases the probability of attendance.

- *Establish a project timeline and procedure for information access*

Outlining the process that the commission will undertake is important. It helps to set the community's expectations and provides a series of short and intermediate goals for the commission and the community. Working with CGR, the JSSCC outlined the entire timeline with the public by working backward from the date that the resolution to consolidate would need to be submitted. This included a list of the many public meetings that the commission envisioned at the end of each point along the timeline and the reports that the commission would create in conjunction with CGR.

Giving the public access to information is critical in any government study. CGR created a website for residents that included all of the commission's work product, reports and meeting minutes. The website built public trust in the process and educated the community on the issues the commission was addressing. Lack of transparency can lead to community mistrust and rumor campaigns can be the death knell for any study.

In addition to the larger public forums, the smaller, personal gatherings/conversations with residents and stakeholders are crucial. The JSSCC established a community outreach subcommittee chaired by resident Carol Golden. The community outreach subcommittee conducted over 70 neighborhood and stakeholder meetings at different milestones in the process - at the beginning, when the options report was presented to the public, and also after the commission made its recommendation to consolidate. The stakeholder meetings were the key to Princeton's consolidation success, because the intimate meetings allowed residents to voice their concerns, ask questions, and provide feedback to the commission in an informal, non-threatening environment.

- *Determine the work product*

The Princeton commission, working with CGR, began with a baseline study. This document served as a foundational analysis of the existing two towns. It determined the debt levels, the assets, and the staffing and services provided by each municipal department. It also provided an insight into the service levels provided in each community. For example, it showed the call volume for the police department in each town and even the frequency of brush and leaf pick up in the borough versus the township. By establishing the existing services and costs for each municipality, the commission created data to evaluate how the towns and/or police and public works departments could be combined. After the baseline report was completed, the commission held a public meeting to review the baseline report. The baseline report created a common starting point for each town's representatives on the commission.

After the baseline report, the commission and CGR produced an options report. Rather than informally discussing potential solutions for the combination of each town's respective departments including police and public works, the options report gave the commission the ability to see the options through a series of lenses ranging from the most conservative approach (with no staff reductions) to the most aggressive approach (staff reductions and potential service delivery changes). The commission was able to have an uncluttered discussion with the community about priorities: cost savings, service enhancements or a combination of both.

Once the options report was released, the commission, through its subcommittees, reviewed each option and determined the most suitable solution for each department. Some options required considerable deliberation, such as the form of government for the new municipality and police department staffing for the combined town. The commission could determine the total estimated cost savings for consolidation by tallying the savings for each of the options it had selected.

The last report was the final report and recommendation from the commission. This report outlined the recommendations, the procedure and timeline for achieving the commission's overall recommendation to consolidate. It also included an analysis of the potential tax impacts from consolidation and an estimate of transition related costs.

- *Conduct a voter outreach campaign*

When the commission made its recommendation to the governing bodies for a consolidation referendum on the ballot, it became imperative that a referendum campaign be formed. If the past consolidation attempts in 1953, 1979 and 1996 were any guide, myths, rumors and a coordinated anti-consolidation campaign could kill the consolidation initiative. Unite Princeton was the critical player that carried consolidation across the finish line with its rapid response to myths and rumors being spread by the anti-consolidation group. The ability to identify voters and help get out the vote contributed greatly to the resounding result of the referendum.

The ghosts of consolidations past left an irrefutable message: the campaign for consolidation had to articulate - proactively - the benefits of consolidation and rapidly dispel myths touted from the other side. Failure to do this would make it nearly impossible to overcome emotions and fear once they have spread through the communities. Any effort on consolidation or shared services that requires voter participation must have a voter outreach effort.

A Final Word

The tale of Princeton's failed efforts and one successful effort to consolidate provides a model and a framework for pursuing similar consolidations and shared regionalization initiatives throughout the state and the nation. A balanced commission, operational by-laws, and a transparent process with a timeline and deliverable work product make it possible to achieve significant cost savings and service enhancements. Public engagement is a part of the process every step of the way and helps to quell concerns and build overall trust in the community.

See the resources in the back of this book for additional information.

Epilogue

Furthering Government Efficiency in New Jersey and Beyond

Consolidation celebrated its third anniversary at the end of 2015. The two municipalities not only stayed together, but also succeeded together.

The blended town of Princeton achieved all of the major promises of consolidation and more. It provided a model for the state and spurred other efforts to reduce the state's layers of government. Phased in over a three-year period, each year's savings exceeded the consolidation commission estimates including the final transition year where the gross savings was $3.9 million. Consolidation savings contributed to the slowing of the town's tax growth rate. Since the merger, Princeton has had a lower tax rate growth than its bordering towns in Mercer County:

Princeton Area Municipal Tax Trends 2010-2015*

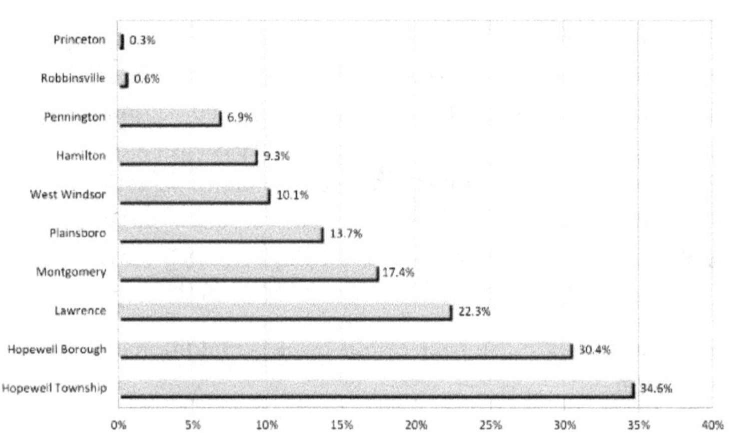

* Based on 2010-2014 Abstract of Ratables for Mercer County & Non-Certified 2015 tax rates; adjusted for Lawrence Twp 2014 revaluation; Montgomery Twp and Plainsboro Twp are preliminary rates for 2015.

2015 Princeton Budget Newsletter

These savings were achieved primarily from staffing reductions by eliminating redundant positions. It is on track to save more money in the future through staff attrition. Furthermore, the municipality saved money in other areas that are hard to quantify but clearly tangible. Princeton optimized its real estate assets by allowing a government-supported nonprofit to repurpose a municipal building no longer housing governmental staff; this saved millions by eliminating the need to acquire new space. Princeton as a united body negotiated a long-term agreement with Princeton University that provided an annual in-lieu of taxes contribution that was greater than the combined borough and township contribution in the year prior to consolidation. The town also renegotiated union contracts, providing additional budget relief and sustainability.

While savings are an important benefit of consolidation, equally beneficial and often overlooked is a more responsive government providing better services to the residents. Princeton now has a much-improved response in clearing roads from storms and managing crisis weather events. It has established Access Princeton, an effective one-stop communications department to respond to residents no matter what their needs.

After over 50 years and a myriad of consolidation attempts, the 2011 vote was historic and proved that it could be accomplished with leadership and community involvement.

Princeton's success has been noticed. Towns like Mount Arlington and Roxbury are exploring consolidation. Others like Chester Borough and Chester Township are looking to make positive changes based on their previous study and have agreed to share police services. There's clearly momentum, but it will take a true movement to continue the progress of eliminating multiple layers of government and inefficiency that hamper savings and service delivery of local governments in New Jersey and around the country.

Consolidation, service regionalization (police, etc.) and other ideas for efficient governance begin at the local government level. To support local officials and citizens in their exploration of consolidation and service regionalization, the state needs to take a leadership role. Prior to our consolidation vote in 2011, the state did step in to offer some transition assistance for the merger. This proved to be an additional boost to the effort. The consensus among other municipal government and school district leaders with whom I have met was that the state needs to be a partner in the process. States should provide financial assistance, legislative flexibility and implementation expertise and guidance in order to make significant inroads into consolidation and regionalization efforts.

Financial Support

We can look to our neighbor, New York State, who, like New Jersey, is faced with a dizzying number of local governments and taxing districts. New York has used state funds to partner with towns and districts to encourage more efficient government structures. The newest fund, called the Municipal Restructuring Fund, provides continuous funding opportunities for towns as they study and implement their consolidation, regionalization or other governmental efficiency efforts.

The process begins with a project charter that outlines a vision and desired goals, scope and potential savings. The state then provides up to $50,000 to get the project off the ground. The State of New Jersey currently has made no funds available for consolidation project initiation.

The state has said that it is reluctant to waste money to fund studies that yield no consolidation. Certain process innovations, however, would encourage towns to move forward with their projects. For example, the state could require that the money given up front is paid back, if the study provides evidence of cost savings and the towns fail to move forward. In addition, the state can provide milestone payment incentives to the project towns along the way – a technique employed by the Municipal Restructuring Fund in New York State. New York has 'project development' and 'small scale implementation' phases that allow the ideas and methodology of the consolidation or restructuring project to be tested with the provision of funds to continue the implementation.

Many studies have gotten off the ground and then have gone off track or been terminated because of changing political control, lack of political will, or opposition. The New York State Municipal Restructuring Fund seeks to overcome those obstacles by partnering with towns and offering financial incentives along each phase of the project as savings are identified and realized.

Legislative Flexibility

The New Jersey Local Option Municipal Consolidation Act was a key piece of legislation that passed while I was in office and allowed us to re-examine consolidation. The flexibility provided in the legislation helps towns get studies off the ground no matter who is initiating - citizens, elected officials or both. Towns can use this law to overcome initial objections to consolidation by enabling them to apportion debt, create separate service districts, delay combining ordinances for continuity and more.

More flexibility, however, is needed. Legislation has been proposed that would allow the consolidation of non-contiguous municipalities. In addition, changes in the law need to permit innovative strategies to overcome potentially divergent tax rates and the effects of tax rate equalization – the biggest obstacle for consolidating. A funding mechanism that helps offset effects from equalizing tax rates exists in the original Local Option Municipal Consolidation Act and it ought to be funded by the legislature (it never was).

Additional legislation could provide more flexible financial mechanisms for towns to offset the initial tax equalization effect. For example, a town could be allowed in a new law to aid the other town's tax base indirectly through debt payoff and state funding incentives – helping to offset the tax rate differential.

We also should be mindful of the potential for more school district consolidations/regionalization. Legislation is needed to help clearly define the process and provide incentives to districts that consolidate.

Expertise and Guidance

Finally, the state should put together a task force that reports to the New Jersey Department of Community Affairs to do the following:

- Proactively review and encourage consolidation and shared services opportunities for municipalities and school districts;
- Provide initial and ongoing strategy and policy support to towns and school districts engaging in a consolidation or regionalization effort;
- Provide recommendations to the state legislature for additional policy changes.

A group whose mission is to identify towns and school districts that are aligned in tax rates, common identity and/or geographic (donut and donut-hole) synergies would be an additional shot in the arm to the consolidation and regionalization effort. For example, publishing a yearly analysis of towns and school districts with relevant financial data that are ripe for consolidation would put additional pressure on towns and districts to consider the idea. It may even help to spur a citizens' effort if the elected officials are resistant to it.

Getting a study off the ground is a major accomplishment. The state's role is to provide a clear understanding of the process; effective study strategies; and rapid response to questions or concerns that arise. Support from a task force of experts will help merger studies stay on track and have a higher probability of reaching a positive conclusion.

Princeton's consolidation has been a shining example in government efficiency and cost savings. The consolidation momentum should be marching forward statewide – with financial incentives and strategic assistance from the governor, the legislature and open-minded local elected officials. Although consolidation never can serve as a cure-all for all of the state's financial woes, local government can be re-invented for cost savings, improved services and strategic planning. The success in Princeton is proof.

About the Author

Chad Goerner

At the age of 21, Chad came to Princeton Township to start a new job. He ended up launching a new town. In 2006 when he walked into his first Princeton Community Democratic Organization meeting in order to meet people and get involved in the community, he had no idea of the impact he ultimately would have on the life of the community.

Chad had no roots in Princeton and never had been involved in or irreversibly traumatized by the consolidation struggles of Princeton's past. His commitment to the cause was born after observing the political and practical dynamics of the two Princetons and then logically concluding that consolidation of the two communities made irrefutable sense. He would dedicate his two terms in office to completing all aspects of a successful consolidation – the first large-scale municipal merger in over a century.

A native New Jerseyan, Chad hails from Wantage Township in northern New Jersey's Sussex County (ironically, Wantage Township attempted to consolidate with Sussex Borough unsuccessfully in 2009). He left New Jersey to go to school - B.A. from George Washington University, followed by the Certified Financial Planner (CFP) designation from the CFP Board and the Certified Investment Manager Analyst (CIMA) designation in conjunction with IMCA and the Wharton School at the University of Pennsylvania.

Chad continues to advocate for policy changes to encourage municipal and school district consolidations and regionalized police and fire services. An expert on the issue of consolidation and shared services, he has delivered numerous speeches and presentations on the subject. He recently delivered the 2016 keynote address to the New York State Local Government Innovation Conference sponsored by the NY Division of Local Government Services.

After his second term ended with the successful consolidation, Chad followed his dream of owning a small farm and moved to Princeton's more rural neighbor Hopewell Township. When not tending to his fruit and vegetable crops or advocating for consolidation and shared services around the state, Chad works as an institutional consultant in the financial industry.

Appendix

I. In Honor – A listing of consolidation commission members from 1952 through 2012

II. Addition Resources – Helpful links and organizations

III. Roles and Responsibilities of a Commission Member – Prepared by the Princeton Joint Consolidation and Shared Services Commission

Appendix I - In Honor

The lists below reflect the membership of the official consolidation commissions dating back to the first commission in 1953. Civic involvement is critical to any effort to change local government and these individuals contributed their time, knowledge and experience for the betterment of the Princeton community.

1953 – Joint Consolidation Committee

Charles T. Cowenhoven, Jr
Joseph J. Redding
Norvell B. Samuels
Raymond A. Bowers
Ralph S. Mason
James A. Perkins

1962 – Joint Committee on Municipal Operations

John B. Redding, Jr.
Orren Jack Turner, Jr.
Gregg Dougherty
James A. Perkins
Dr. William M. Beaney
Stanley C Smoyer
Robert V. Dilley (appointed in April 1963 to serve as Executive Director)
Henry Patterson
Albert Austen
Ellwood P. Godfrey
Kenneth Fairman
Maurice F. Healy, Jr.
William L. Wilson.

1973 – Joint Consolidation Study Committee

Walter Farr Jr.
Barbara Hill
Charles Conforth
Leonard Etz
Allen Porter
Robert Hendry
Lynn Anderson
Helen Fairbanks
Stanley Smoyer
John Galiardo
Robert Sellery
Wood Tate

1979 – Joint Municipal Consolidation Study Commission

Elected Members:

Peter Bearse
Charlotte Gipson
Arthur P. Morgan
William Selden
Nicholas Van Dyck
Jay Bleiman
Margaret Broadwater
Dean W. Chace
James A. Floyd
W. Harry Sayen

1996 – Consolidation Study Commission

Elected Members:

Albert Angrisani
Karen "Casey" Lambert (Hegener)
Claire Jacobus
Margen Penick
Howard Sereda
David Blair
Patricia Cherry
Kay McGrath
Andrea Schutz
Donald Stokes

2010 – Joint Shared Services and Consolidation Commission (JSSCC)

Appointed Members:

Anton Lahnston
Ryan Lilienthal
Mildred Trotman
Patrick Simon
David Goldfarb
Alice Small
Valerie Haynes
Bernard Miller
Chad Goerner
Carol Golden
William Metro

2012 – Transition Task Force

Mark Freda
Hendricks Davis
Bradley Middlekauff
James Levine
Yina Moore
Jo Butler
Dorothea Berkhout
Linda Mather
Scott Sillars
Gary Patteson
Chad Goerner
Bernard Miller

Appendix II - Additional Resources

Princeton Joint Shared Services and Consolidation Commission

Work Materials and Documents:
http://www.cgr.org/princeton

New Jersey Department of Community Affairs
http://www.state.nj.us/dca/divisions/dlgs/

New Jersey Municipal Consolidation Laws:
http://nj.gov/dca/divisions/dlgs/programs/shared_docs/muni_consol_act.pdf

New York State Division of Local Government Services
http://www.dos.ny.gov/lg/

New York State Municipal Restructuring Fund
http://www.dos.ny.gov/lg/lge/municipal-restructuring-fund.html

Organizations:

Center For Governmental Research (CGR)
Dr. Joseph Stefko, President and Chief Executive Officer
1 South Washington Street
Suite 400
Rochester, New York 14614
P: (585) 325-6360
Email: info@cgr.org
Website: http://www.cgr.org

CourageToConnectNJ
Gina Genovese, Executive Director
Email: gina@couragetoconnectnj.org
Website: http://www.couragetoconnectnj.org

Appendix III - Roles and Responsibilities for Commission Members

Prepared by: Princeton Commissioners Alice Small, Patrick Simon, Carol Golden and Anton Lahnston

In 2009, the governing bodies of Princeton Borough and Princeton Township initiated an effort to explore the potential benefits of consolidating into a single municipality or further sharing additional services, specifically police and public works. The Princeton Consolidation and Shared Services Commission was set up to draw on the expertise of elected officials, the administrative staffs of the two municipalities, and an independent consulting firm to provide the research and analysis of the local government structures and a comprehensive assessment of services. The following guidance is based upon the Princeton commission's experience with the roles and responsibilities of commission members.

Commission make-up:

- *Two members from each municipality's governing body.*
- *Three citizens from each municipality, selected by the governing bodies.*
- *Optional alternates from each municipality.*

Specific tasks of a commission:

- *Select an independent consultant.*
- *Prepare a work statement of tasks and manage the work of the consultant.*
- *Work in cooperation with consultant.*
- *Consider and evaluate public input.*

- *Make a recommendation to the municipal governing bodies and community at-large.*
- *Integrate results into a final report.*

<u>The following issues should be included in the final report:</u>

- *A timetable for implementing the plan.*
- *A plan for the disposition of duplicate positions.*
- *Any proposed use of advisory planning districts to provide advice to the planning board and the zoning board.*
- *Any proposed use of service districts comprising the former municipal boundaries to allocate resources and permit continuation of local ordinances that existed prior to consolidation.*
- *Any apportionment of debt between taxpayers of the consolidating municipalities.*

<u>Key attributes of commission members</u>:

- *An open mind to objectively consider the facts.*
- *Commitment to an open and transparent process.*
- *Ability to listen to different and deeply held opinions on emotional issues, while remaining calm and receptive to those opinions.*
- *Ability to make a significant personal time commitment for the following:*

---Preparing for and attending many, often lengthy meetings, at various times during the day, for the entire period of the study.

---Writing minutes and delivering them at public meetings.

---Drafting and commenting on reports.

---Analyzing thoroughly and thoughtfully all the issues presented.

---Serving as a spokesperson for the commission, answering public questions both formally and informally.

Skills, abilities and experience suggested for commission members:

- *Ability to communicate clearly, both orally and in writing.*
- *Active engagement with the community and knowledge of its history.*
- *History of success in public and/or private enterprises.*
- *A commitment to see the process through to the end.*
- *Ideally, no pre-conceived notions about the study. Or have the ability to remain objective when presented with factual data that may be different than one's views.*
- *Experience in municipal government and administration, financial and statistical analysis, legal knowledge, and organizational and leadership experience.*

<u>Recommendations for an effective process</u>

- *Engage an experienced, independent consultant through a competitive process. There needs to be a carefully drafted statement of work to conduct data collection, write reports and to help guide the commission in the selection of options for the future. (Consider a competitive bid process rather than a publicly advertised RFP to avoid the necessity of selecting the lowest priced bidder.)*

- *Establish subcommittees to enable smaller groups of commission members to study in depth and discuss various aspects of the commission's work and make recommendations to the entire commission. Possible subcommittees:*

  - *Police*
  - *Public Works*
  - *Forms of Government*
  - *Finance (Tax and Debt)*
  - *Community Engagement*

(The Princeton Commission attributes its success to the substantive work of the subcommittees and their ability to make strong recommendations to the entire commission.)

- *Make sure to solicit opinions before producing any results. Include in the deliberation and the report of the commission the ideas and concerns that are expressed. Seek to publicly engage early in the process as many stakeholders as possible. (The Princeton Community Engagement Subcommittee had over 60 meetings in neighbors' homes and public venues.)*

Include the following:

---Municipal Employees

---Religious organizations

---Educational institutions (private schools from pre-school to higher education)

---Arts, culture and social organizations

---Merchants' groups and business groups

---Public Policy Groups

---Citizens' groups inlcuding:

-Parent-Teacher organizations

-Senior Citizen groups

-Neighborhood groups

-Ethnic social groups

- *Establish a website as early as possible in the process to keep the public informed. Provide public notice of commission meetings, agendas, meeting minutes and commission reports. In Princeton, the website was established and maintained by the consultant.*

- *Establish(in consultation with the municipalities) a budget for the commission for the following:*

o *Mailings*

o *Printing of reports*

o *Payment to the consultant*

o *Secretary to write minutes and advertise the meetings as required under the Open Public Meetings Act.*

Important recommendations for the commission meetings

The commission meetings are used to update the commission and the public on the progress of the subcommittees' work on the substantive elements of the study. The chair should also use the meetings to provide updates on how much was spent to date against the available study budget.

- *Strong, articulate, well-organized individuals should serve as chair and vice-chair, to provide leadership to the Commission and keep meetings focused and on schedule. They should attend as many meetings as possible.*
- *Publish an agenda in advance of every meeting.*
- *Establish rules of operation, i.e. quorums, how discussions are moderated, etc.*
- *Schedule meetings for at least six months at a time, ideally selecting the same time and place for each with adequate room for the public.*
- *Schedule a few large public meetings over the course of the study to have the consultant present its findings and progress.*

Other recommendations for the consolidation commission:

- *The commission's charter has the option to evaluate both full municipal consolidation, as well as the implementation of additional shared services without municipal consolidation.*
- *The commission should discuss what level of services it will consider, e.g., would it entertain reducing current service levels to achieve savings?*

- *If the commission recommendations are not unanimous, the minority should be strongly encouraged to write a report to explain the reasons why it is dissenting.*

- *The commission should begin to calculate the costs of transition as soon as possible to provide sufficient time for staff to provide estimates (a difficult task and contentious issue).*

- *The financial analysis of consolidation (not just transition) should begin as soon as possible, including early consultation with municipal and county tax officials.*

- *The commission should be encouraged to consult with and direct questions to their Department Of Community Affairs (DCA) representative, who is, by statute, a non-voting member of the commission invited to facilitate the process.*

- *Commission members should review the Princeton Study Commission Final Report on the Other Voices page on CourageToConnectNJ.org*

The Princeton Commissioners offer this guidance to other municipalities contemplating a Consolidation Study process. They are aware that the experiences of other municipalities may be unique.

www.ingramcontent.com/pod-product-compliance
Lightning Source LLC
Chambersburg PA
CBHW070807280326
41934CB00012B/3100

* 9 7 8 0 6 9 2 8 2 9 3 8 7 *